Downhome Blues Lyrics:
An Anthology from the Post-World War II Era

Downhome Blues Lyrics:
An Anthology from the Post-World War II Era

Selected and Transcribed by
Jeff Todd Titon

Twayne Publishers
A Division of G.K. Hall & Co.

Published in 1981 by Twayne Publishers, A Division of G.K. Hall & Company 70 Lincoln Street, Boston, MA. 02111

Printed on permanent/durable acid-free paper and bound in the United States of America.

First Printing

Text and Cover design by Barbara Anderson.

Library of Congress Cataloging in Publication Data
Main entry under title:

Downhome blues lyrics.

  Includes bibliography, discography, and index.
  1. Blues (Songs, etc.)—United States—Texts.
2. Blues (Songs, etc.)—United States—History & criticism. I. Titon, Jeff. II. Series.
ML54.6.D69   784.5'305   81-1174
ISBN 0-8057-9451-4   AACR2

Contents

About the Author

Jeff Todd Titon is an associate professor of English and an associate professor of music at Tufts University, where he teaches American literature, folklore, and ethnomusicology. He holds a bachelor of arts in American Studies from Amherst College, and the master of arts in English and the doctor of philosophy in American Studies from the University of Minnesota. At the University of Minnesota he studied musicology and ethnomusicology with Johannes Riedel and Alan Kagan. His doctoral thesis, "Ethnomusicology of Downhome Blues Phonograph Records," was published in 1977 by the University of Illinois Press as *Early Downhome Blues: A Musical and Cultural Analysis* and won the American Society of Composers, Authors, and Publishers (ASCAP) Deems Taylor Prize. He has received fellowships for research in the blues and in religious folklife from the National Endowment for the Arts and from the National Endowment for the Humanities. He edited a special issue of *Southern Folklore Quarterly* devoted to the blues and is currently serving as record review editor for the *Journal of American Folklore*. From 1969 to 1971 he was the guitarist in the Lazy Bill Lucas Blues Band, with appearances at the Wisconsin Delta Blues Festival and the Ann Arbor Blues Festival.

Preface

Downhome Blues Lyrics: An Anthology from the Post-World War II Era is a collection of outstanding folk blues lyrics composed and sung by black Americans and sold on commercial records in American black communities during the dozen or so years following World War II. To select the lyrics I listened systematically to more than 3000 blues records and transcribed the words of those I thought were the best. I used three criteria. First, I chose only black singers. Although many white singers have recorded blues songs, black Americans invented the blues, nurtured it, and made it a living musical tradition. Second, I transcribed only from recordings originally meant for the black communities. This limited the selections to commercially recorded 78 and 45 rpm records and ruled out the albums blues singers made for the urban white middle class during the folk music revival of the late 1950s and early 1960s. Third, I evaluated the lyrics' merit, selecting those that made the transition from song to the printed page with grace and meaning. In the blues musical culture the chief criterion of a song's worth is how true the words are to the real and imagined experience of its listeners. Of course any song performance is more than its lyrics; much is lost when a song is transformed to words printed in verse. Because blues is music for dancing as well as listening, many songs that sound good and feel good in performance look trite on the page. But many that appeal in performance also read exceptionally well on the page and in my view take their place among the outstanding lyrics in the English language.

It should be obvious that blues research cannot progress without reliable and accessible collections of authentic blues song performances. In 1968 when I began selecting and transcribing lyrics for this book no serious and comprehensive collections of downhome blues lyrics, whether postwar or prewar, commercial or field-collected, had been published. Since that time two worthy anthologies have appeared. *Living Country Blues* is an anthology of 221 blues song lyrics (some printed with tunes) collected in the field from singers in Louisiana during 1955–61 by folklorist Harry Oster.[1]* *The Blues Line* is an anthology of 274 blues song lyrics selected and transcribed by Eric Sackheim from prewar commercial downhome blues records.[2] The present anthology differs from *Living Country Blues* in that the lyrics represent commercial recordings made for a black audience—not field recordings made for a folklorist; it differs from *The Blues Line* in that the lyrics represent the postwar period when a new generation of blues singers spoke for the secular side of the black experience.

Notes to the Preface will be found on page 195.

Acknowledgments

I am grateful to the copyright owners for permission to print my transcriptions of several of the song lyrics in this anthology; I credit them individually in the Notes to the Lyrics. Record collectors Joe Grosz, Bob Koester, Leroy Pierson, Mike Rowe, Chris Strachwitz, Bruce Bastin, Frank Scott, and Pete Welding are among those who made my task of locating postwar downhome blues records easier by reissuing many of them on albums (see pp. 199–203). David Evans and John Barnie checked my transcriptions and supplied some second opinions. My parents, Edith and Milton Titon, helped me locate copyright claims. My wife Paula and daughter Emily were infinitely patient while I worked on this project. The National Endowment for the Humanities supported my research on this book with a Summer Stipend in 1974.

Portions of the Introduction appeared earlier in different form. I am grateful to the American Folklore Society for allowing me to reprint parts of my article, "Thematic Pattern in Downhome Blues Lyrics," from the *Journal of American Folklore* 90, no. 357 (1977). I wish also to thank Robert S. Thomson, editor of *Southern Folklore Quarterly*, for permission to reprint parts of my introduction and the article, "Every Day I Have the Blues," from that journal's special blues issue, vol. 42 (1978).

Introduction

The music of black people in the New World has a rich and glorious history. Neither African nor European, nor a mixture of the two, it is a fully black American music, varying with place and time to give voice to changes in black people's ideas of themselves.[1]* Whether found in North America, South America, or the Caribbean, and despite the different forms and styles evolved in the past few centuries, it has retained a core of ecstasy which, for the participant, transforms the regularity of everyday life into the freedom of expressive artistry.

In this century the black musical style revolutionized popular music in the United States—the music of the theatre, movies, radio, and television. Music on 78 rpm records from around the turn of the century sounds stilted, extravagantly dramatic, shouted and jerky because of the period influence of marching band music and grand opera. In the 1920s, aptly called the Jazz Age, Bessie Smith and other black blues singers radically changed the art of singing popular music. Their approach was close to the rhythm and tone of ordinary talk, and their natural way of singing caught on. Popular music was never the same again.

The blues is therefore a familiar music, but its familiarity presents problems, chiefly the misconception that blues is a sub-type of jazz, a contributing stream that flowed (shortly after Bessie Smith died) into the river of jazz. But the blues is a music of its own. Blues is best understood as a feeling (the blues) and a musical form, whereas jazz is a technique, a *way* of forming. Inevitably jazz musicians applied their technique to the blues, but the blues's identity and the musical culture associated with it have remained distinct. Until the late 1950s, when desegregation and the Civil Rights Movement

---

Notes to the Introduction will be found beginning on page 195.

altered black social and economic conditions, the blues musical culture, with singers who specialized in blues songs, country juke joints and barrelhouses, city house and rent parties, street singing and bar scenes, nightclubs and lounges, recordings and record industry, was a major part of the black musical culture in the United States. Today, despite predictions of its impending death—predictions that have come regularly for the past sixty years—the blues culture continues to flourish.

The music I call *downhome blues* is sometimes called *country blues* by other writers. The terms may be used interchangeably—as blues singers use them—for the same music is under discussion. But since country blues was (and is) sung and played in towns and cities by people who grew up there—particularly in the post-World War II era—the term *country* is misleading. The term *downhome* is evocative, calling up not so much an actual, physical place (the country), but the *spirit* of the place, which moved with the music and culture as blacks carried their downhome way of life into the twentieth-century cities. It is this feeling or spirit that singers, listeners, and dancers affirm is at the heart of the downhome blues musical experience.

The postwar blues era—roughly, the dozen years after World War II—was marked by a resurgence of downhome blues. The wartime factories in Chicago, Detroit, Los Angeles, and other cities paid well and induced a mass migration of farm families from the South and Southwest. The black farm families brought with them much of their downhome way of life: food, religion, music. Inevitably, city life made new demands on the people, while the cash-wage economy made a new life possible. Record companies foresaw a large market, many new companies formed, and they recorded a great variety of black music. The urban blues, jazz, and "jump" tunes appealed to a sophisticated audience. The texture of this music suggested the complexity of urban life and the ghetto-dwellers' growing mastery over it. The companies also recorded downhome blues and gospel songs cast in an older mold that appealed to working-class blacks who remained in the rural South or had recently migrated to the factory cities but felt most comfortable with a downhome way of life. These records document experiences and attitudes of a segment of American society, black working-class men, who have otherwise left little for the humanist historian. Moreover, as musical literature the records are vital and strong; the world their lyrics fashion is rich and moving.

Downhome blues lyrics pass judgment on human behavior and show how to get along in the world. Most of them are dramas of love in which the singer casts himself as a mistreated victim. He introduces an antagonist (mistreater) and, as he describes his mistreatment, draws up a bill of indictment. Then, with the listener's tacit support, the victim becomes the judge, and the drama turns on the verdict: will he accept the mistreatment, try to reform the mistreater, or simply leave? Resigned acceptance and attempts at reform resolve only a minority of downhome blues lyrics. Most often, the victim, declaring his independence, steps out of his role with an ironic parting shot and leaves.

Although blues songs do not narrate stories as ballads do, the entire body of blues lyrics constitutes a story: a cycle of journeys in search of fair treatment and better times. Broadly reflecting the history of millions of black Americans who migrated after Emancipation from one farm to the next and then to the towns and cities, the story's irony mirrors their attitude toward progress. Within the larger story cycle, each song, sometimes each stanza, becomes a way-station, a temporary resolution that will give the singer strength to begin again. While the theme of many Anglo-American folk ballads is romantic tragedy (love thwarted by fate, ending in death) the theme of black American blues is the ironic comedy (a victim celebrating his fragile, newly-asserted freedom). The pattern of Anglo-American balladry is linear, progressive, and final; the pattern of the blues is cyclical and regenerative. The section headings for the lyrics in this book ("Down Home," "I'm the Sweetest Man in Town," etc.) move sequentially through one such cycle; the lyrics take their organization from this larger story.

As a musical genre the blues has been in existence since the 1890s, but musicologists and literary critics have only recently realized that blues lyrics comprise a literature of merit and interest. Reasons for the delay in recognition include racism as well as Western civilization's tacit preference for the written word over oral tradition. Older upper- and middle-class blacks were hostile to a music they associated with poverty, violence, sexual license, and irresponsible behavior; the younger, politically radical blacks identified the blues with passivity and resignation in the face of racial discrimination. Finally, the folklorists and musicologists who might have gathered, preserved, and championed the blues on its merits remained ambivalent toward a music that many thought had been contaminated by professional entertainers, the mass media, and commercial exploitation.

Several encouraging signs from the past decade indicate a change in attitude. The blues is a vital part of the black experience and cultural identity. Interpreting the blues as a music of resignation is to mistake the mask for reality. At the core of the blues is freedom from mistreatment, not submission to it. Black poets have found continuing inspiration in the heritage of the blues, and black literary critics have turned to the blues as an expression of the black aesthetic. Stephen Henderson's *Understanding the New Black Poetry*, probably the decade's outstanding contribution to black literary criticism, draws heavily on blues and the black oral tradition.[2] Blues songs now occupy an important place in the histories of black American music, and in the histories of American music.[3] Blues lyrics increasingly claim their place in the canon of American literature. A selection of blues lyrics appears, for example, in *American Literature: The Makers and the Making*, one of the current, widely-used textbook anthologies of American literature. The editors of that anthology, Cleanth Brooks, R. W. B. Lewis, and Robert Penn Warren—and it would be difficult to find a more distinguished trio of American literary historians—conclude a seven-page prefatory essay on blues as follows: "In the world of music the recognition of blues as art is well established. But waiving their value as musical art, we may assert that they represent a body of poetic art unique and powerful. The world they spring from is totally recreated—no, created, with its drama, comedy, pathos, and range of feeling. No body of folk poetry in America—except, perhaps, the black spirituals—can touch it, and much of the poetry recognized as 'literature,' white or black, seems tepid beside it."[4]

The final indication of a new attitude toward blues songs lies in the changing conception of folklore itself. An earlier generation of folklorists considered folksong to be a separate entity, distinct from popular music (associated with professional entertainers, the profit motive, and mass media) and from classical music (associated with elite groups, written musical scores, and unvarying performances). Folksongs were defined as traditional music that passed by ear and imitation from one singer or instrumentalist to the next, changing words and tunes as they went and, over time, giving the music the stamp of the community; the age and folk-quality of a folksong could be determined from the multiple versions collected. Folksongs flourished in rural, pre-industrial areas among an illiterate peasantry; literacy, industrialization, and urbanization were regarded as enemies of folk tradition. This definition, while useful, could not account for the persistence of folksong among close-knit ethnic groups in modern cities; it also placed undue emphasis on the idea that a folksong was in essence a text with a tune. Folklorists today conceive of a folksong as a performance, not an item, whose meaning and folk-quality arises from what it communicates in the performance situation.[5] In other words, a song with the same text and tune may be folk in one context but not in another. When a concert singer includes "Barbara Allen" in a recital at Carnegie Hall, the context does not yield a folksong.

Current thinking in the field of folklore emphasizes that folksongs reflect the informally shared experience of a group of people (the folk group) closely linked by one or more common bonds such as occupation, neighborhood, social class, ethnic heritage, church affiliation, dialect, race, age, political outlook, sex, and so forth. Folksongs are songs that are shared among folk groups as events in the home or community gathering places where most people present take an active role, interacting with one another as listeners, dancers, or performers. Popular music differs from folksong because it detaches its audience from the performance. The raised platform of the concert stage symbolizes the separation of performer and audience, as does the acoustically isolated musician's booth in the recordings studios, where producers and engineers quite literally manufacture popular music from interchangeable parts. The audience buys popular music as a commodity, whether on record or in concert. Popular music is a product to consume. Folk music is an event to share.

As the thinking about folksong changed to emphasize the folk group and the performance context, folklorists and musicologists realized that within some folk groups community-based, professional entertainers perform and carry folksong traditions. Certainly this has always been true in the blues music culture, where the working-class black men and women of the farms and factories formed folk groups that recognized outstanding singers by giving or bartering food, drink, money, or other possessions or services in

Ex. 1. "Candy Kitchen."

"Candy Kitchen"—(Sam Hopkins)© 1971 Modern Music Publ. Co.   Used by permission.

↑ indicates a pitch slightly higher than notated but insufficiently high to be properly notated by the next chromatic step.

↓ indicates a pitch slightly lower than notated but insufficiently low to be properly notated by the next chromatic step.

〰 indicates a slur or glide between two pitches (measure 6 and also the pick-up measure) or downward to an indefinite pitch (measure 3).

exchange for the singers entertaining at picnics, parties, dances, in taverns, nightclubs, or homes.[6] In the post-World War II era, when these local entertainers stepped inside the studios to record the downhome blues songs that are collected in this anthology, they provided a permanent inventory of folk tunes, lyrics, and arrangements—the sound of blues music.

I Blues as a Musical Form

Jazz musicians "play the blues" (without lyrics) as a melodic and harmonic mold into which they can pour a variety of tunes, yet in essence the blues is a type of vocal song that, while sharing attributes with other song types, has several identifying features of its own. Among these are its historical development, context and style, and the artistry of its lyrics (which will all be discussed subsequently). The blues also has a characteristic structure (melodies, harmonic patterns, verse forms) that renders the music unmistakeable.

Blues lyrics are usually set in three-line or quatrain-refrain verse forms. In the *three-line verse form* (Ex. 1; transcription 56) the second line repeats the first, sometimes with slight variation, while the third completes the thought with a rhyme:

> Yes these is awful things, just to hear a black man say.
> Yes these is awful things to hear a black man say.
> Yes you know I done throwed my shovel away 'cause I
> don't have to work on that W.P. and A.

My preference is to write the three-line verse in six half-lines:

Yes these is awful things
Just to hear a black man say } *1st line, made up of 2 half-lines.*

Yes these is awful things
To hear a black man say } *2nd line (2 half-lines)*

Yes you know I done throwed my shovel away 'cause I don't*
have to
Work on that W.P. and A. } *3rd line (2 half-lines)*

---

line should continue but page prevents it from doing so.

The advantage of transcribing it in six half-lines is the transference to the page of the singer's timing, for blues singers almost always pause at the half-line divisions. In this type of transcription—which has come to be known as *ethnopoetic transcription*—the printed page becomes a field across which sounds and silences move proportionately in time. In this book, a new line at the left margin indicates a short pause after the previous line ("Yes these is awful things"—pause—"Just to hear a black man say"—longer pause—"Yes these is awful things"). A new line starting where the prior line ends signifies a very short pause:

<blockquote>
If you don't I'm

      going to

            have to go
</blockquote>

The example shows very short pauses after "I'm" and "going to." In this ethnopoetic transcription, punctuation that serves the purpose of showing stops is superfluous and hence omitted. If the reader will move his eyes from left to right across the page, pausing at the line breaks, he will have no trouble reading in a way that resembles the singer's rhythm.

In the postwar blues era one additional verse form is important: a rhymed quatrain (four half-lines) followed by a two-line refrain. I term this the *quatrain-refrain verse form*. It can be compared with the three-line verse form directly in those blues songs such as "Money, Marbles and Chalk" (Ex. 2; transcription 19) which exhibit both verse forms. The first verse (in ethnopoetic transcription):

In the evenin'
After the sun goes down } *1st line*

In the evenin'
After the sun goes down } *2nd line*

The womens all tell me
I'm the sweetest man in town } *3rd line*

Ex. 2. "Money, Marbles and Chalk."

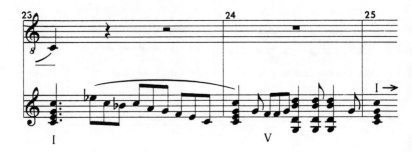

↑ indicates a pitch slightly higher than notated but insufficiently high to be properly notated by the next chromatic step.

⌐ indicates a slur or glide between two pitches (measures 1, 2, 5, 6, 10, 17, 18, 21, 22) or downward to an indefinite pitch (measure 2).

𝖝 indicates an unstable pitch in the region notated.

This is the standard three-line verse form. But the second verse is in the quatrain-refrain form:

> Now I've got a little woman
> She's got money marbles and chalk
> She bought me a fine Cadillac man   *quatrain*
> Now I don't have to walk

> In the evenin'
> After the sun goes down
> The womens all tell me   *refrain*
> I'm the sweetest man in town

Comparison reveals that each verse form occupies 12 measures and that the refrain of the quatrain-refrain form is identical to the second and third lines of the three-line form. These two verse forms account for approximately nine-tenths of the lyrics in commercially recorded, postwar downhome blues songs. The other tenth is more or less free in form, with a variable number of lines sung or spoken (or both) to an accompaniment that remains on the tonic triad.

Ex. 3. The blues scale.

↑ indicates a pitch slightly higher than notated but insufficiently high to be properly notated by the next highest chromatic step. The arrows identify the "neutral" third and tenth.

Δ indicates the important pitches in the blue note pitch complexes.

The scale appears in the key of C for convenience.

Blues melodies are built from a scale that blues songs share with other black American folk and popular song types. The outstanding feature of the blues scale (Ex. 3) is its inclusion of both major *and* minor thirds, major and minor sevenths, major and minor tenths, and perfect and flatted fifths. The range of the scale is a tenth rather than an octave because the tenths are used differently than their counterparts, the thirds; for example, the major third is sung more often than the minor, but the minor tenth is sung more often than the major. In addition, the blues scale contains neutral thirds and tenths, distinct pitches about halfway between the major and minor. That is a relatively great amount of tonal material, particularly the clusters of pitches around the third, fifth, and seventh, and tenth degrees of the scale. These clusters are usually termed the *blue note*. Since, however, each cluster is a series of pitches used in characteristic ways, I prefer to think of the degrees as pitch regions and to treat each series of pitches in those regions as a "complex" or related group of pitches.[9]

The harmonic support for blues melodies is supplied by the accompanying instruments. For the first four measures of the 12-measure strophe, the accompaniment is based on a tonic chord, usually a tonic triad for the first three measures and the tonic seventh for the fourth measure. (Sometimes in the second measure of the 12-measure strophe the accompaniment is based, as in "Money, Marbles and Chalk" [Ex. 2 meas. 2], on the subdominant triad.) Measures 5 and 6 are based on the subdominant triad, usually creating tension with the melody, which remains the same as in measures 1 and 2 when it was supported by the tonic. The accompaniment in measures 7 and 8 returns to the tonic; measure 8 usually adds the tonic seventh. Measure 9 is supported by the dominant or dominant seventh chord, and measure 10 by the subdominant or subdominant seventh. In many prewar and in fewer postwar downhome blues songs, however, the accompaniment remains on the dominant or dominant seventh throughout both measures 9 and 10. Measure 11 rests on the tonic, and measure 12 sometimes moves to the dominant seventh, leading to the tonic at the start of the next 12-measure strophe. The basic structure of postwar downhome blues song accompaniment is illustrated in Ex. 4, a skeleton of Ex. 2. Urban blues and jazz musicians modify this harmonic structure with altered chords and chord substitutions. Because this is an anthology of blues lyrics, further analysis of blues melodies is beyond the scope of this Introduction; but the reader is referred to my *Early Downhome Blues* for a comprehensive treatment that proceeds from analysis to synthesis and shows how blues melodies are generated from their component parts.[10]

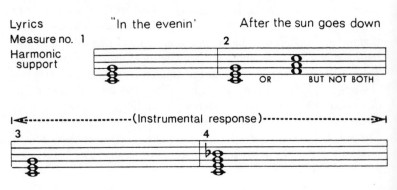

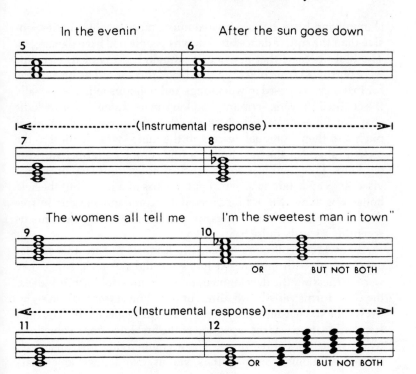

Ex. 4. Structure of 12-measure, 3-line downhome blues strophe, showing harmonic support and placement of vocal "call" and instrumental "response." Given in key of C for convenience.

II Blues Music to World War II

The origin of blues cannot be traced to a specific composer, date, or location. One might just as well try to trace the invention of blueberry pie. The blues was not born fully formed; rather, it evolved gradually from earlier black song types until it possessed the characteristic style, structure, and social context that gave it its identity.

The best evidence indicates that the blues began as community-based, secular dance music during the 1890s.[11] New dances like the shimmy and black bottom invited music more flexible and responsive than the square dance breakdowns people had been dancing to. The blues became that new music, although many of its elements were borrowed from older types of black folksong. The blues scale, for instance, was used in worksongs and religious music, especially the chanted prayers, sermons, and long-meter hymns. The melodic shape of blues—repeated phrases with a sharp rise to the highest pitch and then a gradual descent to the tonic—was identical to the melodic shape of the field holler, a solo sung by a farmer working outdoors. Like the blues song, the field holler consisted of improvised lines and stanzas, often about the loss of a lover. But the field holler was sung without instrumental accompaniment and in free rhythm, while the blues songs were accompanied by instruments accenting a steady pulse beat.

About 1900, collectors of black folk music noticed this secular dance music with improvised lyrics but did not realize that they were witnessing the development of a new musical form.[12] Indeed, the verse forms varied: two, three, or four-line verses took on eight, twelve, or sixteen-measure strophe patterns respectively. The only standard feature was the repetition of the first line—once, sometimes twice, sometimes three times. The accompanying instruments in these earliest blues songs—guitars, violins, mandolins, banjos, harmonicas, and other portable instruments—were confined to the tonic chord throughout, repeating ostinato patterns in response to the singer's phrases. The collectors did not call these songs blues, and we may therefore suppose that the singers did not either; if they had, the collectors surely would have reported it. Yet it is clear from the collections of black folk music and the reminiscences of musicians of that era that the blues in all likelihood began in the 1890s, and that it was known in communities along the Mississippi River and its southern tributaries by 1900.

The evolution of blues music continued prior to World War I with four important developments. The first was a gradual consolidation of blues songs toward three-line verse forms with twelve-measure strophes and the harmonic pattern of tonic-subdominant-tonic-dominant-tonic (Ex. 4). The second was the spread of blues throughout the South and Southeast, particularly in the rural areas. Since the improvised lyrics could be strung together over a solid, vigorous beat for a long time, the blues was an ideal music for dancing and listening. It was especially attractive to the singers because they could make up their own songs. A third development was the growth of blues in black stage shows. Touring black bands as well as vaudeville, minstrel, and medicine shows featured soloists with blues songs in their routines. These songs, composed by black, professional tunesmiths, have come to be known as *vaudeville blues*. Meanwhile the country dance parties that featured local and itinerant blues singers continued the now-established tradition of downhome blues. The fourth important development was a national blues craze that began when W. C. Handy's compositions, "The Memphis Blues"(1912) and "St. Louis Blues" (1914), spread from black to white popular culture through live performances, sheet music, and recordings by white singers and bands. Broadway professionals and out-of-town amateurs rushed to capitalize on this "new" music. After the United States entered World War I the blues craze ended, but in black America both the vaudeville and downhome blues remained staples of the musical diet.

By 1920 the blues had become the most popular type of secular music for black Americans. Black singers and musicians now made the first blues recordings.[13] The sophisticated, vaudeville blues was recorded first, sung by women with show backgrounds and accompanied by pianists or small jazz combos. The best of these entertainers, Ma Rainey and Bessie Smith, were enormously well received; their records sold well, to white people as well as black, and their singing styles strongly influenced—indeed, revolutionized—American popular music. The vaudeville blues of the 1920s is also known as the *classic blues* in recognition of its achievement. Recording of the downhome blues began in the mid-1920s. Sung mainly by men accompanying themselves on guitar or piano, the songs reveal the dominance of the three-line verse form and harmonic support (Ex. 4); other verse forms were recorded as well, showing that the consolidation and standardization of the blues from a structural viewpoint was incomplete. The record companies sent portable recording equipment to Southern cities and financed country musicians' trips to Northern studios, obtaining a variety of regional and local blues singers and unwittingly documenting the folk blues tradition.

The downhome and vaudeville blues records were a success, both artistically and commercially. During the Depression of the early 1930s, however, the record companies reduced the amount of black music recorded, eliminating the field trips to the Southern cities and relying instead on musicicians living in the North. The rise of jazz music turned popular attention from vaudeville singers and toward jazz bands; as the black stage show tradition declined, so did vaudeville blues. Meanwhile, despite the cutback in recording activity, the downhome blues tradition continued vigorously in the South, where the Saturday night dance parties were an institution, and in the northern cities, where migrants from the South brought their music and culture into the black ghettos. Some of the downhome music from the rural South was documented on field recordings for the Library of Congress, while a small number of outstanding downhome blues singers, such as Tommy McClennan and Robert Johnson, made commercial recordings. This rough-and-ready music, with its improvised stanzas and riff accompaniments, surfaced late in the decade in several of the Kansas City and Territory jazz bands. Blues "shouters" (as they were called) boomed their voices over the sound of big jazz bands, gaining regional and national exposure on records and radio. Walter Brown, Hot Lips Page, and Jimmy Rushing were among the better known blues shouters, and Count Basie's was the best-known band. This blues was the prototype of the *urban blues* of the 1940s and 1950s, a sound and style to be contrasted with postwar downhome blues in Section III.

The United States' total involvement in World War II had a significant impact on the black musical culture and in retrospect appears as a watershed. Shortly before the war, James Petrillo, president of the musicians' union (the American Federation of Musicians), forbade members to make records.[14] He believed that record sales and juke boxes were making it more difficult for musicians to obtain live entertainment bookings. The Petrillo ban and wartime shortages of shellac (the material from which records were made) halted the commercial recording of blues during the war and many of the musicians interrupted their lives to enter military service. Nonetheless, the blues traditions continued in the local communities while military jazz bands and blues shouters spread the music internationally, to Europe and the Far East. When the war ended and the Petrillo ban was lifted, the blues and jazz traditions were still the outstanding outlet for the new talent in the black musical culture. A new generation of jazz musicians innaugurated the be-bop era in jazz. Blues shouters saw their music develop into urban blues and rhythm 'n' blues. And new migrants from the South appeared in Los Angeles, Chicago, Detroit, Houston, Memphis, and other cities to strengthen the downhome blues scenes there.

III Postwar Blues Music

The singers who made downhome blues recordings in the postwar period shared broadly similar personal histories. A close look at the early life and career of one of the most prominent among them, Muddy Waters, will help in understanding the background and social context of postwar downhome blues.

Waters was born McKinley Morganfield to sharecropping parents in Rolling Fork, Mississippi. When his mother died a few years later he was sent to live with his grandmother in Clarksdale. Hating the tedium of farm work, he saw in music an alternative to debt and drudgery; music would be a way out, a way to make a name for himself, and a calling. "I always thought of myself as a musician," he said. "The jobs I had back in Clarksdale and so forth, they were just temporary things. I still considered myself . . . well, if I wasn't a good musician then, I felt that sooner or later I would be a good musician. I felt it in me."[15]

He learned the rudiments of blues singing in the time-honored downhome way. His grandmother took him to church on Sundays; he was moved by the music of the hymns, the tone of the chanting preacher, the sung prayers, and the rhythms of the congregational response. "I had it in my mind even then to either play music or do something that I would be well known," he said. "I was a good old Baptist, singing in church. A hard shell Baptist (ha ha). So I got all of my good moaning and trembling going on for me right out of church."[16] He took up harmonica, then guitar, and began singing the folk songs and blues that the local musicians performed on the streets, at picnics, and at country suppers. He said, "I really admired music so much—but if they was singing good blues, I just loved 'em. But my copy was Son House. He traveled through the area and lived on a plantation too—one way across from me. He didn't never be still like me, 'cause he'd do a lot of traveling all over the Delta. And any time I could get a chance to hear him play, I'd go."[17] Waters was fortunate in having Son House and Robert Johnson to copy (formal lessons did not exist) because they were recognized masters of downhome blues, traveling to provide entertainment at the Saturday night parties and making commercial phonograph recordings. (After Johnson was murdered, Waters studied his records.) The blues singers' chief concern was learning to play the music. They preferred to make up their own words but they also absorbed a great many lines and verses from the singers they imitated, thus perpetuating a common stock of lyrics in oral tradition.

Soon Waters was singing and playing guitar in a local string band, shouting over the noisy crowds in the juke joints, playing at suppers and barbecues, and singing on the streets on Saturday afternoon when everyone came to town. He provided the same sort of entertainment as countless other local musicians throughout the rural South. Recordings document this stage in his musical development: when Alan Lomax and John Work came through the Mississippi Delta in 1941 to record Robert Johnson for the Archive of American Folk Song, they were told that Johnson was dead but that Waters would make a good substitute. In 1941 and 1942 Lomax recorded Waters and the members of his string band. Most of his songs, such as "I Be's Troubled," were traditional and contained stanzas from the common stock, but into many of them Waters mixed original stanzas, giving them his personal stamp.[18] Singers considered a song original if it contained two or more stanzas they believed they had invented. Had Waters remained in the Delta, he would have enjoyed increasing local fame, perhaps eventually traveling, like his mentor, Son House, from one plantation to the next, stopping in several of the larger towns, and occasionally reaching a city; but opportunities for recording and establishing a wider reputation seemed limited. Many people were migrating north from the Delta, where the wages were higher and jobs more plentiful during the war years. Even Son House had taken a job with the railroad and moved to Rochester, New York. So Waters, encouraged by Lomax's attention, decided to head north. "I wanted to get out of Mississippi in the worst way," he said. "I figured if anyone else was living in the city I could make it there, too."[19]

In 1943, with only his guitar, suitcase, and an extra suit of clothes, Waters moved to Chicago and stayed with friends and cousins while he found a job in a corrugated-paper carton factory and looked for work as a musician. Soon he had enough money to get an apartment of his own, but finding a job as a singer was difficult. "In music then you'd go in and tell the people you played blues; a lot of 'em they'd shake their head and say, 'Sorry, can't use you.' "[20] Downhome blues was considered old-fashioned. Its singers could not compete for bookings in the sophisticated nightclubs where cocktail jazz trios like Nat Cole's, smooth vocal groups like the Ink Spots, and jump combos like Louis Jordan's put forth a sound more restrained and tightly organized than the downhome singers could produce. Gradually the downhome singers found work in the rougher clubs and neighborhood bars in the urban ghettos and surrounding industrial towns. To be heard above the noisy crowds, they amplified their instruments electronically. The postwar era is marked by this shift from acoustic to electric blues. Instrumental techniques did not change, but the sound had a raw edge to it, a new energy. The people liked it.

Shortly after the war, the major record companies lost interest in recording blues. Meanwhile, several small, newly-formed record companies broke the major companies' monopoly on black music. Since a best-selling record could turn an enormous profit from a relatively small investment, the owner-producers of record companies experimented with music they thought might sell. Among the music they recorded (though by no means dominant) was the downhome blues they found in the neighborhood joints. "When I first saw Leonard Chess in 1946," reported singer Lazy Bill Lucas, "he had a tape recorder [and was] going around from tavern to tavern looking for talent."[21] Although Chess recorded a variety of music, his most successful singer was Muddy Waters, whose 1948 commercial recording of "I Be's Troubled" (which Lomax had recorded in 1941 as a folk song) sold more quickly than Chess could supply it to distributors. While driving at night and delivering venetian blinds (he could not subsist on his musical earnings), Waters heard his recorded voice blasting out of apartment windows. "I used to wonder if I had died," he said.[22]

Downhome blues records, sold to blacks in the South as well as in the urban North, Midwest, and Far West, never captured a very large share of the market. Most people preferred the modern blues sounds of cocktail crooners like Charles Brown or the more complex big band arrangements that sometimes showcased blues shouters like Wynonie Harris, Joe Turner, T-Bone Walker, or B. B. King. Blues singer Baby Doo Caston ascribed the difference between downhome and urban blues to social status:

Blues is the thing that if it was done a certain way everybody liked it. And Billy Eckstine came out with Earl Hines's band singing, 'Jelly, jelly, jelly stays on my mind,' and most everybody bought the record because a big band was right behind it. But if it had been somebody like Sonny Boy Williamson with his harp [harmonica] and somebody playing them old guitars behind him, an old bass, and beating on a drum, they wouldn't have bought it because it was kind of a gutbucket thing. It's just the style of it; it was a class.[23]

Postwar downhome blues differed from urban blues in sound as well as in class context. Whether coming from a big band or a cocktail jump combo, the modern urban sound was precise and finely detailed, the instruments arranged hierarchically, each with its distinctive range, riff, and tone color. The elegance of that sound—the sense of great power held in easy restraint—suited the atmosphere and expected behavior at a cocktail lounge or supper club. The downhome blues, on the contrary, often sounded blurred, the instruments blending in egalitarian indistinctness as piano, guitar, and harmonica sometimes doubled each other's riffs, pouncing in response to the vocalist's phrase. The downhome sound was well suited to the rugged bar atmosphere in which it flourished as well as the makeshift storefront and garage studios in which it often was recorded. Downhome blues singers and their bands were not schooled in the precision, the complex harmonic structures, and the plenitude of the urban blues sound; they stayed instead in the well dug groove of the three-chord (tonic, subdominant, dominant) format.

The differences in lyrics and singing style also reflected the contrasting urban and downhome traditions. Usually relying on professional songwriters, the urban singers, heirs to the vaudeville blues singers of the 1920s, used the familiar conventions of pop and novelty pieces to push against the limitations of the basic blues structure; their lyrics reflected a Broadway legacy of self-directed irony and a certain coyness. The recorded lyrics of downhome blues singers displayed more originality and thematic coherence than would a typical evening's session in a neighborhood club. For their lyrics in performance, they relied on a stock of traditional songs and stanzas, renditions of current recordings, songs of their down-the-street competitors, and a small supply of original songs which passed into tradition as other singers learned them from performances and from records. Irony in downhome blues lyrics abounded, though it was rarely self-directed; most often it was reserved for the mistreater character. Urban blues vocalists crooned and shouted; downhome blues vocalists confined themselves to a narrower dynamic range. Because urban blues lyrics fitted precisely into the common twelve-measure strophe, musicians could anticipate their entrances and perform their parts with precision. The downhome singer, who usually accompanied himself, was not so careful. If he held a line for one or two extra beats, if he shortened the musical time between lines, or if he lost his place during an instrumental break, he expected his sidemen to follow him. As a result, the downhome blues songs sometimes exhibit eleven, eleven-and-a-half, twelve-and-a-half, and thirteen measure $\frac{4}{4}$ (or $1\frac{2}{8}$) strophes, and occasional confusion among the accompanists.

There are individual exceptions to these distinctions between urban and downhome blues styles in the postwar era but, as a whole, they outline clearly audible differences that in turn reflect contrasting attitudes toward the demands and pace of city life upon people who not long ago were farmers. Downhome blues steadied the recent migrants; urban blues appealed to those who had made the transition successfully.

IV Lyrics: Meaning and Significance

Freedom is the overarching theme in postwar downhome blues lyrics. (It is a major theme in prewar lyrics as well.) The large number of songs concerned with motion, journeys, and anticipation suggests that freedom is at the heart of their expression. The overt subject matter of many songs, mistreatment (and what the singer will do about it), allows the singer to express his desire for freedom more concretely.

The singer of a blues song casts himself in the conventional role of mistreated victim. Because of that convention we cannot assume that the words—whether traditional or original—speak personally for the singer. (Sometimes, of course, they do.) Movement is precipitated in downhome blues songs by a mistreater, a character who does not respect the singer's dignity. Sometimes the mistreater is an authority figure, such as the plantation owner, the factory foreman, or the grocer who sells the singer's family their food on credit. Most often the mistreater is a lover and since most downhome blues singers are men (class and context again), the mistreating lover is usually a woman.

The occasion for the song is the recognition of mistreatment. The plantation owner may want to work the sharecropper so hard that he refuses him the time to bury his wife: "That white man says, 'It's been raining. / Yes and I'm way behind. / I may let you bury that woman one of these old / Dinnertimes.' "[24] Perhaps the foreman fires the singer: "I went to work this morning, / Was all set to start. / My boss walked up and told me / Something break my heart: 'Things so slow / Don't think we need you any more."[25] The mistreating lover may spend all the singer's money: "You know she takes my money, / She calls me 'Jack.' / She holds her hands out for it, she never give it back. / She's a money-taking woman."[26] She may come home drunk after a night's partying: "My baby went out last night and got drunk, / Came home raisin' sand. / She had nerve enough to tell me, 'L. C., / I found me a brand new man.' "[27] She may sleep with another lover: "Now you know my mm-baby she didn't go no place / But to church and the Sunday school. / But now she run around in every notoriety joint in town / And have every man she meet."[28] She may not care enough to manage the household: "Yes, house it ain't never clean. / My supper it ain't never done."[29]

The singer offers evidence of the mistreatment and enlists the sympathy of the listener; the drama turns on how the singer will respond. The situation confronts him with a choice: either try to make the best of a bad situation, attempt to reform the mistreater, or leave. Sometimes the singer imagines another way out— murder— but almost always he comes to reject that alternative.

If the singer chooses to reform the mistreater, he may give advice:

"Well you run all up and down the street, / Running other women's men. / You better take it easy, baby. / Take it easy while you can 'cause your time— / Baby you know your time ain't long."[30] He may also direct his advice to the woman's sense of responsibility: "Please come home to your daddy / And explain yourself to me / Because I and you is man and wife / Trying to start a family. / I'm begging you, baby, / Cut out that off-the-wall jive."[31] The professed reformer may even admit he shares the blame: "Baby you got to help me get myself straightened up right now. / If you don't I am / going to / have to go."[32] But downhome blues singers usually do not admit fault, nor do they realize that the mistreating lover may justifiably be liberating herself from his care and control.

Accepting mistreatment confirms the downhome blues singer in the role of victim. Sometimes the victim role seems inescapable, particularly when economic conditions are to blame: "Well I left home this morning, boys, you know / 'Bout half-past nine. / I passed the stockyard, you know the boys were still / On the picket line. You know I need your hundred dollars."[33] The singer may accept his fate with a proverbial expression: "Now if you don't have no money, peoples, / You can't live happy no more."[34] More often, his response includes irony: "Yes you know I bought her a radio; / I even bought her a 'lectric fan. / She said, 'Sam, I'm gon' lay here and God knows I won't have no other man. That made me feel so good / Till I don't know what to do. / Yes, darlin, every dollar poor Sam makes, you know, / He got to bring it back home to you."[35] Occasionally, his response is threatening: "Yeah, got so mad this morning, / Broke to the wall right through there. / Grabbed my shotgun, I started to / Mow that woman down."[36]

Most often the victim resolves the drama of mistreatment according to the third alternative: he frees himself, reestablishing his dignity by leaving, as, for example, in the following lyric.[37]

"Mistreated Blues"

1. I been mistreated so long
   Babe it seems like my time ain't long

   I been mistreated so long
   Babe it seems like my time ain't long

Yeah you know if that woman don't come back this time
You can bet your last dollar the poor girl is dead and gone

2. Now I'm gonna carry my old shotgun
   B'lieve I'll take along my forty-four

   Now I'm gonna carry my old shotgun
   B'lieve I'll take along my old forty-four

   'Cause honey you done dogged me long enough
   I declare you won't dog me no more

3. Ever since I been in love with you
   Wolf's been hollering all in my door

   Ever since I been in love with you
   Say the wolf's been hollering all in my door

   Yeah this is your last time now baby
   Swear you won't dog me no more

4. Now goodbye baby
   I declare I'm going down the line

   Yes bye bye baby
   Honey I declare I'm going down the line

   Yes you can have your troubles in this world
   Babe I declare I'll have mine

"Mistreated Blues" opens with a general complaint about the lover's absence. The singer, who addresses the listening bystander in the first verse, turns a threat toward the lover in the second as he states his intention to search for her, gun in hand. A complaint cast in the proverbial expression, "wolf's been hollering all in my door," continues the threat in the third verse. Perhaps these words are muttered while the singer, carrying his gun, seeks his lover. The threat turns out to be empty, and in the final verse the singer announces his decision to leave. As he addresses his lover once again, we may suppose he has found her, either in this verse or in the previous one. Instead of shooting her, he declares his independence from her: "You can have your troubles in this world; / Babe I declare I'll have mine." He ironically suggests that it will be better to endure the inevitable "troubles" separated from one another.

An ironic parting characterizes a great many downhome blues lyrics, and often it displays the compression of proverbial expression: "I like you all right, baby, / But I just can't stand your ways"[38] or "I'm going upstairs; / I'm going to bring back down my clothes. / If anybody asks about me, / Just tell 'em I walked outdoors."[39] Sometimes the parting is angry: "It took me a long time / Long time to find out my mistake (it sure did, man) / But I'll bet you my bottom dollar / I'm not fattening no more / frogs for snakes."[40] Irony takes note of lessons learned but also shows the singer's ambivalence, for the mistreating lover remains an object of desire: "Yes you know she's a sweet little girl / But I'm gonna have to let her go."[41]

Whether the mistreater is boss or lover, the relationship is exploitative, as this widely-sung lyric makes plain.[42]

"Five Long Years"

1. If you've ever been mistreated
   You know just what I'm talking about

   If you've ever been mistreated
   You know just what I'm talking about

   I worked five long years for one woman
   She had the nerve to put me out

2. I got a job in a steel mill
   A-trucking steel like a slave
   For five long years every Friday I went straight home with all*
       my pay if you've
                       Ever been mistreated
   You know just what I'm talking about

---

*line should continue but page prevents it from doing so.

I worked five long years for one woman
She had the nerve to put me out

3. I had a death in my family
She wouldn't give me a helping hand
I borrowed two or three dollars from the woman she said hurry*
    up and pay it back old man if you've
                        Ever been mistreated
You know just what I'm talking about

I worked five long years for one woman
She had the nerve to put me out

4. I finally learned a lesson
I should have known a long time ago
The next woman I marry has got to work and bring me some*
    dough

I've been mistreated
You know just what I'm talking about

I worked five long years for one woman
She had the nerve to put me out

In "Five Long Years" the mistreating lover has forcibly freed the
singer. Nonetheless this victim envisions reversing roles on the next
potential mistreater. The frequency with which the singers state
that they have worked hard for a woman and have given her their
earnings bespeaks the transference of the relationship from boss to
lover.

Exceptional downhome blues artists carry the ironies of paternalistic treatment satisfyingly far. *Tim Moore's Farm*, by Lightnin'
Hopkins, provides an example. Plantation owner Tim Moore was
known for feeding his sharecroppers unexpectedly well on surprise
occasions: "Soon in the morning, / He'll give you scrambled eggs;
/ Yes but he's liable to call you so soon you'll catch a mule by his
hind legs."[43] Whether Moore was generous or unkind, the abrupt-

---

line should continue but page prevents it from doing so.

ness of his actions confirmed that he controlled his sharecroppers at his whim. In a lyric which comments ironically on New Deal liberalism, the same artist, Lightnin' Hopkins, asserts his dignity by throwing away his WPA shovel even though this means conforming to a black stereotype.[44]

"Candy Kitchen"

1. Well I don't work in no candy kitchen little girl
   God knows I don't sell no chewing gum

   I don't work in no candy kitchen little girl
   God knows I don't sell no chewing gum

   Yes but still I don't have to grab no pick and shovel woman and
   Roll from sun to sun

2. Yes I woke up this morning
   Man the rain falling on the ground

   Yes I woke up this morning
   Boy the rain falling on the ground

   Yes I had to go work for the W.P. and A. and boys you know*
      it's
   Way over crosstown

3. Yes these is awful things
   Just to hear a black man say

   Yes these is awful things
   To hear a black man say

   Yes you know I done throwed my shovel away 'cause I don't*
      have to
   Work on that W.P. and A.

---

line should continue but page prevents it from doing so.

In this splendid lyric, the singer gives his distaste for a long walk in rainy weather as an excuse for leaving his job. As he talks to his lover, however, he reveals that the nature of the WPA work itself is the problem. Work in a candy kitchen is the "little girl's" naive view of paradise; his WPA job, to "roll from sun to sun" with pick and shovel, is like prison work. The triviality of his excuse supports his pose: the nonchalant fellow to whom such a job means little. But a source of wages during the Depression is not easily dismissed as trivial. The final verse gets at the heart of the matter; unlike a prisoner, he is not forced to dig ditches and to break rocks. To him such work is demeaning, and rejecting it asserts his freedom. The ironic word *awful* contrasts the difference between the popular interpretation of his act as lazy and irresponsible with its true meaning—he throws his shovel away in an act of defiance.

Freedom from racial discrimination is not a widespread theme in downhome blues lyrics. The blues is simply not a major outlet for racial or social protest. The eloquence of songs like "Candy Kitchen" and "Tim Moore's Farm" is enhanced by the theme of social injustice but does not derive from it. Rather, the exploitative situations provide blues singers, who are best understood as artists, not social critics, with the opportunity to explore a universal human theme and to make it specific through the black experience. Blues lyrics offer a great deal more than lament. Whether concerned with lovers or bosses or both, they dwell on the complexities of human entanglements and the recurring necessity to be free of them.

Lyrics

A Note on the Symbols

Each of the following lyrics is the complete recorded text. When I have had to guess the words, I have italicized them. Lines below blank spaces indicate that a good guess could not be made. Words that are spoken rather than sung appear in parentheses. I have numbered each verse consecutively. The unconventional placement of the texts and the elimination of unnecessary punctuation reflect the singer's rhythm (see Introduction, pp. 7-8). An asterisk (*) indicates that the line should continue but the page prevents it from doing so.

I

Down Home

"Well I'm a down home girl,
And I'm tired of fooling with you."

—*Memphis Minnie, "Down Home Girl" (transcription 115).*

1. DOWN IN MISSISSIPPI

1.   Down in Mississippi where
             Cotton grow tall
             Get arrested for trouble you got to
             Call the hound dog
                             oh uh
      Down in Mississippi
      Whoa yeah where the cotton grow tall

      Yes and on the other hand baby
      Boll weevil wearin' overalls

2.   Go to work in the mornin' you know
             'Bout four o'clock
             Uh if the mule don't holler you
             I don't know when to stop
      Down in Mississippi baby
      Uh whoa yeah where the cotton grow tall

      Well and on the other hand baby
      Boll weevil wearin' overalls

3.   I go to church in the mornin' baby you know
             Down the railroad track
             Late over in the evenin' they bring
             Bring the preacher back
             He eat up all the chicken now but uh
             Right to the neck
             Look over at my baby and
             He eat up the rest 'cause he was
      Uh down in Mississippi
      Uh oh yeah where the cotton grow tall

      Well now and on the other hand baby
      Boll weevil wearin' overalls

                                        —Jimmy Reed

2. HAVE YOU EVER

1. Have you ever been way out in the country
   Peoples during the harvest time

   Have you ever been way out in the country
   Peoples during the harvest time

   Pickin' fruit and draggin' a big fat sack of cotton
   And the sun beaming down your spine

2. At noon I fall up under some shade tree
   Tryin' to figure what move to make

   At noon I fall up under some shade tree
   Tryin' to figure what move to make

   Well _____ I'm right back down between two middles
   Tryin' to get my numbers straight

3. If I ever get from around this harvest
   I don't even want to see a rose bush grow

   If I ever get from around this harvest
   I don't even want to see a rose bush grow

   And if anybody ask me about the country
   Lord have mercy on his soul

—Mercy Dee

3. BIG BOSS MAN

1. Big boss man
   Can't you hear me when I call

   Big boss man
   Can't you hear me when I call

Well you ain't so big
You just tall that's all

2.   You got me workin' boss man
         Workin' round the clock
         I want a little drink of water
         So that you won't let Jimmy starve big boss man
Can't you hear me when I call

Well you ain't so big
You just tall that's all

3.   Well I'm gonna get me a foreman
         One gonna treat me right
         Work hard in the daytime
         Rest easy at night big boss man
Can't you hear me when I call

Well you ain't so big
You just tall that's all

—Jimmy Reed

4. GROSEBECK BLUES

1. Boy you may go to Grosebeck to have your trial
   But you know the _____ penitentiary's after while

   You may go to Grosebeck to have your trial ooh
   And the _____ penitentiary's after awhile

   Yes if you want to go to penitentiary in a hurry man
   You just go to Grosebeck and have your trial

2.   Yeah you know my mama called me
         Boys and I answered"Ma'am?"

She said 'Son are you tired of working?" I said*
  "Mama
Oh mama yes I am"
Then you know my papa called me
Peoples and I answered "Sir?"
He said "Son if you're tired of workin' down there
What the hell you're gonna stay there for?"
Grandma said "Son if you had been a good boy
Yes and stayed at home
You'd have been workin' for your mama I'm*
  talkin' about and pickin' up *chips* on your*
  grandma's farm"

I can't do nothin'
But hang my lonesome head and moan

3.   Yes you know they got a dog named Rattler
You know she's a water dog
You know she can swim big Brazos I done swear*
  man that dog can walk a foot log

—*Lightnin' Hopkins*

5. TIM MOORE'S FARM

1. Yeah you know it ain't but the one thing
You know this Black man done was wrong

Yeah you know it ain't but the one thing
You know this Black man done was wrong

Yes you know I moved my wife and family
Down on Mister Tim Moore's farm

---

line should continue but page prevents it from doing so.

2.   Yeah you know Mister Tim Moore's a man
            He don't never stand and grin
            He just said "Keep out of the graveyard I'll
            Save you from the pen" you know
    Soon in the morning
    He'll give you scrambled eggs

    Yes but he's liable to call you so soon
    You'll catch a mule by his hind legs

3.   Yes you know I got a telegram this mornin' boy it*
                read
            It say "You're wife is dead"
            I show it to Mister Moore he said "Go ahead nigger
            You know you got to plow old Red"
            That White man says "It's been raining
            Yes and I'm way behind
            I may let you bury that woman one of these old
            Dinnertimes" I told him "No Mister Moore
    Somebody's got to go"

    He says "If you ain't able to plow Sam
    Stay up there and grab your hoe"

                                        —*Lightnin' Hopkins*

6. TROUBLE AT HOME BLUES

1. I've got roaches in my kitchen
   Mouses like a growed up coon

   I've got roaches in my kitchen
   Mouses like a growed up coon

   Look like these rats and roaches
   Goin' to drive me out of my room

---

line should continue but page prevents it from doing so.

2. They keep rippin' and runnin'
   People I can't rest at night

   They keep rippin' and runnin'
   People I can't rest at night

   For these rats and roaches
   Eating up my meat and rice

3. The rats runnin' in my kitchen
   The roaches is 'round my cab'net door

   The rats runnin' in my kitchen
   The roaches they's 'round my cab'net door

   These rats done got so brave 'round here people
   They shut the gas off on my stove

—*Silas Hogan*

7. BURNIN' HELL

1. Well ever'body's talkin' 'bout that
   Burnin' hell
   Ain't no heaven or
   Ain't no burnin' hell
   Where I die where I go
   Nobody tell I say
   Yeah ever'body talkin'
   'Bout this burnin' hell
   (Yes
   Yes)

2. Well mama told me
   And papa did too
   "Go down to the church house now son get on your
   Bended knees

Ask Deacon Jones just to
Pray for you I say
Ask Deacon Jones
Oh Lord to pray for you"
I found
I *done* found
I went to the church house
On bended knee
Told Deacon Jones I said uh
"Pray for me"
Deacon Jones said now said
"Here's my hand
Yes now children now now now
I'm goin' yes yes
Pray for you if I don't
Never pray no more"

Yeah Deacon Jones
He prayed that morning

3. Yes I done prayed
   I done sung
   Did ever'thing that a poor man
   Sure could do well I
   Ain't gon' pray no more

—John Lee Hooker

8. BAD BOY

1. I used to be a bad boy a bad boy
   Don't have to be bad no more

                          oh well

   I used to be a bad boy
   Don't have to be bad no more

   I learned my lesson
   A long
          time ago

2. My mother died
   Left me
         by myself
   My mother died
            oh well
                  she left me by myself

   Well well well well well wel-ll-ll mmmmm mmm m mmm
   Now I ain't got nobody
   Set down and talk with me

3. Ohh
      mmmmmm mm mmm mm
                   Lord Lord
   Lord I'm by myself
   My brothers
         and my sisters
               don't seem to know me
                       Lord*

    no more
  Mm mmm mm mmm mm mm

                          —*John Lee Hooker*

9. COTTON CROP BLUES

1. Ain't gonna raise no more cotton
   I'll tell you the reason why I say so

   Ain't gonna raise no more cotton
   Tell you the reason why I say so

   Well and you don't get nothin' for your cotton
   And your seed's so doggone low

Line should continue but page prevents it from doing so.

2. Well like raisin' a good cotton crop
   Just like a lucky man shootin' dice

   Well like raisin' a good cotton crop
   Just like a lucky man shootin' dice

   Work all the summer to make your cotton
   When fall comes it still ain't no price
   (Oh now
   Oh help me pick right here boys
   Oh yeah
   So dark and muddy on this farm)

3. I have plowed so hard baby
   Corns got all in my hands

   I have plowed so hard baby
   Corns have got all in my hands

   I want to tell you people
   It ain't nothin' for a poor farmin' man

—James Cotton

10. DARK MUDDY BOTTOM

1. Walked down so many turnrows
   I can see them all in my sleep

   I walked down so many turnrows
   I can see them all in my sleep

   Sharecroppin' down here in this dark muddy bottom
   With nothin' but hardtack and sorghum to eat

2. Four-thirty and I'm out in the barnyard
   Tryin' to hook up my poor beat-out raggedy team

   Four-thirty and I'm out in the barnyard
   Tryin' to hook up my poor beat-out raggedy team

All of my stock is dyin' of starvation
And my boss is so doggone mean

3. Now there's got to be some change made around here*
     people
I'm not jivin' that's a nat'ral fact

There got to be some change made around here people
I'm not jivin' that's a nat'ral fact

I'm gonna jump up on one of these old poor mules and
     start ridin'
And I don't care where we stop at

—Mercy Dee

11. DOWN CHILD

1. Down child down child
I been down all of my days
                              oh well

Down child down child
I been down all my days

I need somebody to help me
Oh Lord
          Lord I ain't got no home

2. Highway
Highway highway
Have been my home
Well
Who been
Callin' my name

---

line should continue but page prevents it from doing so.

I been pushed around people
From door to door
Ain't had nobody
To feel for me
Oh Lord
Please somebody
Please help me
Out of the
Shape I'm in
Well
Oh Lord
My baby gone

3. Oh Lord oh Lord
   Oh Lord people mm
   I ain't got no home
   Got no shoes
   On my feet
   Been travelin'
   I'm travelin'
   Down child
   All of my days

—John Lee Hooker

II

I'm The Sweetest Man In Town

"In the evenin'
After the sun goes down,

The womens all tell me
I'm the sweetest man in town."

—*Jimmy Rogers, "Money, Marbles and Chalk" (transcription 19).*

45

12. SHE FOOLED ME

1.   I went out walking
          Full of my good gin
          A lady was in the doorway she
          Asked me in
          Said if I would sweep her kitchen
          And move her furniture 'round
          I could pick up on what she
          Would put down but she fooled me
       Yes she fooled me

       Well that woman she fooled me
       Jivin' me all the time

2.   I cleared her kitchen
          I dust' out ev'ry crack
          I mowed that woman's lawn from the
          Front to the back
          She promised me a kiss and then she
          Promised me a hug that if I would
          Clean her kitchen it'd be
          Out her dining room rug but
       She fooled me
       Yes she fooled me

       Well that woman she fooled me
       Jivin' me all the time

3.   I asked that woman for to let me be her kid
          She say "You
          May get bold and you may not keep it hid"
          She looked at me and then she
          Slyly smiled she said "I
          B'lieve I'll try you for my kid man awhile"
       But she fooled me
       Yes she fooled me

       Well that woman she fooled me
       Jivin' me all the time

4.   The next time I saw that lady
            She invited me to her home
            She told me she didn't have no husband
            She was living alone
            I axed about a little lovin'
            She told me it was strictly fine
            Yet she said "You've gotta have the money daddy*
                because
            I've got the time"
            I gave her forty-five dollars
            And taken her to be my friend
            Before things could get on their way
            Her husband he walked in then
She fooled me
Yes she fooled me

Well that woman she fooled me
Jivin' me all the time

—Harvey Hill, Jr.

13. EVIL BLUES

1. People I'm black I swear I'm evil
   I'm just as evil as a man can be

   People I'm black I swear I'm evil
   I'm just as evil as a man can be

   You know I don't care if nobody in this whole round world
   Oh baby now ever think of me

2. My daddy he was a preacher
   My mother she was sanctified

---

*line should continue but page prevents it from doing so.

You know my daddy he was a preacher
And my mother she was sanctified

Well now you know I must've been born the devil
Because I didn't want to be baptized

3. I don't want no jet black woman
   Because she is evil too

   You know I don't want no jet black woman
   Because she is evil too

   You take when two evil people wake up early in the*
      mornin'
   Oh man there ain't no tellin' what they may do

—*Lil' Son Jackson*

14. MATTIE MAE

1. Hello stranger
   Sure do remind me of Mattie Mae

   Hello stranger
   Sure do remind me of Mattie Mae

   And if you should ever need a favor
   Call on Baby Boy right away

2.   Now Mattie Mae's only five foot two
             And her hips is kind of wide
             She ain't no great big woman but you know she*
                on the heavy side
   Hello stranger
   Sure do remind me of Mattie Mae

---

*line should continue but page prevents it from doing so.

And if you should ever need a favor
Call on Baby Boy right away

3.   Now you just Mattie Mae's complexion
        And you're just her height and size
        You walk bowlegg'd just like her you know you*
            got those dreamy eyes

Hello stranger
Sure do remind me of Mattie Mae

And if you should ever need a favor
Call on Baby Boy right away
(All right Calvin)

4.   Mattie Mae ain't so good looking
        And her teeth don't shine like pearls
        But the Lord has give her something you know*
            that takes her through this world

Hello stranger
Sure do remind me of Mattie Mae

And if you should ever need a favor
Call on Baby Boy right away

5.   If Mattie Mae tell you that she love you
        You can bet she'll treat you right
        She will help you when you're down and she don't*
            like to clown and fight

Hello stranger
Sure do remind me of Mattie Mae

And if you should ever need a favor
Call on the old boy right away

—*Baby Boy Warren*

---

*line should continue but page prevents it from doing so.

15. GOIN' FISHIN'

1. Ain't no need of sittin' down thinkin' baby 'bout
   Some of the things run 'cross my mind

   I was sittin' down thinkin' baby 'bout
   Some of the things run 'cross my mind

   Ain't no need to go fishin' baby
   Honey when you only take a line

2.   I went fishin' one day baby take
            A line and no pole
            When I thought about it baby I was a
            Very sorry soul yeah then just sittin' here thinkin'
   Some of the things run 'cross my mind

   Ain't no need to go fishin' darlin'
   When you only take a line

3.   Know they said the fish was bitin' baby didn't
            Even need a hook
            When I got out there baby all I
            Got was a dirty look then I'm sittin' down thinkin'
   Some of the things run 'cross my mind

   Ain't no need to go fishin' darlin'
   When you only take a line

                                        —*Jimmy Reed*

16. KISSING IN THE DARK

1.   Call the doctor
            Call him quick
            I done got something 'bout to make me sick I been*
               kissin' in the dark

---

*line should continue but page prevents it from doing so.

Yes kissin' in the dark

Kissin' in the dark
Honey that's my birthmark

2.   Well I had a girl friend from Alabam'
        She done put her business all in a jam
Kissin' in the dark
Yes kissin' in the dark

Kissin' in the dark
Honey that's her birthmark

3.   She had a date with a *square*
        She met a hip cat
        And nobody knows where she end up at she been*
            kissin' in the dark

Yes kissin' in the dark

She been a-kissin' in the dark
Honey that's her birthmark

4.   Real good pals been swapping our dimes
        You thinkin' 'bout my man throw it out your mind
Kissin' in the dark
Kissin' in the dark

Kissin' in the dark
Honey that's my birthmark
(Yes let's get it now)

5.   Well you better wake up
        And try to get wise
        Get yourself hip to that old crazy jive
Kissin' in the dark
Kissin' in the dark

Kissin' in the dark
Honey that's my birthmark
(I done told you)

                                        —*Memphis Minnie*

---

line should continue but page prevents it from doing so.

17. PLEASE DON'T THINK I'M NOSEY

1.
    Good mornin' little beautiful darlin'
    Wait just a minute don't get me wrong
    Are you expecting some private party
    Or you just standing all alone but lady please*
        don't think I'm nosy

I'm just as kind kind as I can be
I know that the present of your future
Bears the whole world and all to me

2.
    I would like to ask some information
    Are you gonna make this town your home
    May I extend my conversation
    Or would I have to keep movin' on but lady*
        please don't think I'm nosy
I'm just as kind kind as I can be

Because the present of your future
Bears the whole round world to me

3.
    Now let's you and I get acquainted
    Tell me what might be your name
    Don't think I'm tryin' to find out your 'rangements
    But darlin' who's your lovin' man but lady please*
        don't think I'm nosy

I'm just as kind as I can be
I know that the present of your future
Bears the whole round world to me

(Darlin' don't think I'm nosy because I'm askin' this but I*
    just can't help it)

4.
    If you don't have no objections
    We'll go out and drink and dine

---

*line should continue but page prevents it from doing so.

I would like to ask a few more questions
Can I possibly call you mine but lady please don't
    think I'm nosy

I'm just as kind kind as I can be
Because the present of your future
Bears the whole round world to me

—Baby Boy Warren

18. BAKER SHOP BOOGIE

1.   I got a little girl got a baker shop
    Jelly roll's the highest thing she got just the baker*
        shop boogie
Yes the baker shop boogie

Yes the baker shop boogie it's the nicest thing around

2.   She got muffins and *scones* she got corn bread too
    Sweet rolls and jelly boys I'm really tellin' you yes*
        the baker shop boogie

Yes the baker shop boogie
She got the baker shop boogie it's the nicest thing in town

3.   She got her own flour she mix her own dough
    Without my sugar she just can't go yes the baker
        shop boogie

Yes the baker shop boogie

Yes the baker shop boogie it's the nicest thing around

4.   I walked in the bak'ry thought ev'rything was sold
    I found out she saved me some sweet jelly roll yes*
        the baker shop boogie

---

line should continue but page prevents it from doing so.

Yes the baker shop boogie
Yes the baker shop boogie it's the nicest thing in town
(All right let's boogie some)

5.   If you want some suger you really
           Want it sweet
           Walk in to the bak'ry 'bout the middle of the*
              week it'll be the baker shop boogie

Yes the baker shop boogie
Yes the baker shop boogie it's the nicest thing in town

                                                     —*Willie Nix*

19. MONEY, MARBLES AND CHALK

1. In the evenin'
   After the sun goes down

   In the evenin'
   After the sun goes down

   The womens all tell me
   I'm the sweetest man in town

2.   Now I've got a little woman
           She's got money marbles and chalk
           She bought me a fine Cadillac man
           That's why I don't have to walk in the evenin'

   After the sun goes down

   The womens all tell me
   I'm the sweetest man in town

---

line should continue but page prevents it from doing so.

3.   I've got a little woman
          She's just as sweet as she can be
          I wants the whole world to know
          She's all right with me when in the evenin'
     After the sun goes down

     The womens all tell me
     I'm the sweetest man in town

—Jimmy Rogers

20. ROUGH DRIED WOMAN

1. I got a rough dried woman
   Never finish anything she starts

   Yes I got a rough dried woman
   Never finish anything she starts

   Now my woman lives in the city but she's country way*
      down in her heart

2. She gets up early in the mornin'
   Just about the break of day

   Yeah she get up early ev'ry mornin'
   Just about the break of day

   She can't be a farmer's daughter 'cause she only does*
      things half way

3.   She hugged me
                    she kissed me
          Till my liver reached the peak

---

line should continue but page prevents it from doing so.

   She said "Hold on Mac
   I'll be back next week"
   I got a rough dried woman
Never finish anything she starts

Now my woman live in the city but she's country way*
   down in her heart

4. Oh baby
   You're a rough dried woman
   You're just like coffee baby
   Without cream or sugar

                    oh yes you is

   You're just like bacon baby
   All alone on a plate

5. But I got a rough dried woman
   Never finish anything she starts

   Yes I got a rough dried woman
   Never finish anything she starts

   My woman live in the city but she's country way down in*
   her heart

6. And ohh baby
   You're no good
   But let me tell you one more thing
   You're just like starched clothes on a line
   But come on in this house woman
   And let me see can I iron you out
   But come on
   It's all right
   Come on baby

                              —*Big Mac*

---

line should continue but page prevents it from doing so.

21. ALLEY SPECIAL

1. You know now mama take me out to the alley now mama
   Before the high water rise
   Y'all know I ain't no Christian
   'Cause I
           once have been baptized know I went to church*
     this mornin'
   Yes and they
               called on me to pray
   Well I fell down on my knees
                           on my knees
   Gee
       I for—
           forgot just what to say

2. You know when I cried "Lord my father my Jesus" I*
     didn't know what I was doin'
   I said that would be the kingdom come
   I say if you got any brownskin women in heaven
   Will you please to send Wright Holmes one
   Listen master you
                   know I ain't never been to heaven
   Oh *there's a black one*
                       I have been told
   You know they tell me got women up there
                               women up*
       there
   Gee with their mouths all lined with gold

3. I'll bet you I get my cream from a cream'ry .
   You get your'n from a jersey cow (all right)
   I'll bet you I'll get my meat from a pig

---

line should continue but page prevents it from doing so.

I'll bet you get your bacon from a no-good sow tell the*
    truth now don't you because the woman I'm gon' to*
    lovin'
She's a holy woman
                              and she
                                    beats that tambourine
And ev'ry time me and that little sister go to lovin' each*
    other
Oooh well boy
                    she talks that *only one* tongue to me

4. You know I 'cided to get me nigh a little heifer
   And I'm gonna get me one little jersey bull
              Lord don't you hear me now mama
              Keep on a-talkin'
   Yeah I 'cided to get me nigh a little heifer
   Yes I'm gon' get me one little jersey bull
   I'm gonna keep on a-churnin' churnin'
   Yeah
         till my
                    churnin's done got full
   (Well I believe I'll churn a little bit
   Yeah)

5. Now some of these here days
   I'm gonna have me a heaven of my own
              Lord don't you hear me
              Keep on a-pleasin' to you
   Babe I say some of these here days
   I'm gonna have me a heaven of my own
   I'll have a gang of these brownskin women
         Yeah they're gon' be gathered all 'round my throne

                                        —*Wright Holmes*

---

*line should continue but page prevents it from doing so.

22. LONESOME CABIN

1. In my one-room
               little cabin
                       just me and my
                                 little
                                    girl alone

   In my one-room
               little cabin
                       just me and my
                                 little
                                    girl alone

   It makes a man
               feel so good
                       when she wrapped way back*
       in your arms

2. The little room is so small
                       I can't even put up no cookin'*
       stove

   The little room
               is so small
                       till I can't put up
                                 no uh cookin'*
       stove

   But you can tell
               from the weather
                       it's so c$_{o}$l$_{d}$
                                 uh cold*

       outdo$_{o}$r$_{s}$
   (Walk
   Mm hmm)

---

line should continue but page prevents it from doing so.

3. I could hear it rainin'
                    and see the lightnin'
                                    flashin' on my
    uh windowpane
Yes rainin'
                could hear it rainin'
                                and I could see the
        lightnin'* flashin' on my
                            uh windowpane
But the little girl laid her head
                            upon my chest and said I*
        love you and I'm
                    I'm not ashamed

—*Sonny Boy Williamson*

23. EYESIGHT TO THE BLIND

1. You're talkin' about your woman
   I wish to God man that you could see mine

   You're talkin' about your woman
   I wish to God that you could see mine

   Ev'ry time the little girl start to lovin'
   She bring eyesight to the blind

2. Lord her daddy must been a millionaire
   'Cause I can tell by the way she walk

   Her daddy must been a millionaire
   Because I can tell by the way she walk

   Ev'ry time she start to lovin'
   The deaf and dumb begin to talk

---

line should continue but page prevents it from doing so.

3.   I remember one Friday mornin' we was lyin' down*
           across the bed
         Man in the next room a-dyin'
         Stopped dyin' and lift up his head and said "Lord
Ain't she pretty
And the whole
                state know she fine"

Ev'ry time she start to lovin'
She bring eyesight to the blind
(All right 'n' all right now
Lay it on me lay it on me lay it on me
Oh Lordy
What a woman what a woman)

4. Yes I declare she's pretty
   And the whole state knows she's fine

   Man I declare she's pretty
   God knows I declare she's fine

   Ev'ry time she starts to lovin' whooo
   She bring eyesight to the blind
   (We got to get out of here now
   Let's go let's go let's go now)

                              —*Sonny Boy Williamson*

24. GOOD NEWS

1.   I got a letter this morning my wife had a brand*
           new baby girl
         When I got the news I was
         Halfway 'round the world that's good news

---

line should continue but page prevents it from doing so.

Whoa boys that's good news

Whoa boys that's good news
What my baby said

2.   Well you know I'm leavin' in the mornin'
        I'm on my way home
        When I get there I'm gon' rock that
        Woman in my arms that's good news
Whoa boys that's good news

Whoa ho boys that's good news
What my baby said
(Look out
Whoa do it again)

3.   Well you know I'm gon' give away candy I'm gon'*
            have
        Cigars for sale
        I know she love me
        And boys she wouldn't fail that's good news
Whoa boys that's good news

Ho ho boys that's good news
What my baby said

4.   Well you know soon as I get home I'll rock that*
            baby on my knee
        Reach over and kiss her mother and say, "Girl you*
            can't be beat" that's good news

        Whoa boys that's good news

        Ho ho boys that's good news
        What my baby said

—*Muddy Waters*

---

line should continue but page prevents it from doing so.

25. MR. HIGHWAY MAN

1. (Wow! Better watch out man how you drive that Cadillac*
      there.
   I'm tellin' you.
   Ain't that a fine machine?)

   Drive your automobile down the highway man on the road

   Drive that automobile there that man's on the road
   (Who is that? That's a policeman.)
   You better drive right careful
   On this highway route

2.   Green light says stop
           Red light said go
           Looka there man there's a man on the road that's a*
              highway man
   Parked on the road

   You better drive that Cadillac
   You better drive it right on the road

3. Oh mister man
   "Please check my oil"

   Oh mister man
   "Please check my oil

   I've got a two hundred to go and I'm *foulin'* _____ "

4. This here Cadillac is a long ragged machine
   This here Cadillac is a long ragged machine
   Me and my baby can ride and ev'rything'll be good to me

                                        —*Howlin' Wolf*

---

line should continue but page prevents it from doing so.

26. SANTA CLAUS

1. My baby went shoppin' yesterday
   Say "I'm gon' buy what you need for Santa Claus"

   My baby went shoppin' yesterday
   And say "I'm gon' buy what you need for Santa Claus

   I'm gon' take mine with me
   But I'll leave yours in my dresser drawer"

2. So that started me to ramblin'
   Lookin' in all of my baby's dresser drawers

   Well that started me to ramblin'
   Lookin' all in my baby's dresser drawers

   Tryin' to find out
   What did she bought me for Santa Claus

3. When I pulled out the bottom dresser drawer
   The landlady got mad and called the law

   When I pulled out the
                           bottom dresser drawer
   The landlady got mad and called the law

   I was just tryin' to find
   What did she bought me for Santa Claus

4. The police walked in and *touched* me on the shoulder
   "What you doin' with your hand in that woman's dresser*
       drawers?"

   I hand the police a letter my baby
                                   wrote me
   Showin' where should I find my Santa Claus

---

line should continue but page prevents it from doing so.

I just kept on
Pullin' out all of my baby's dresser drawers

5. I walked out left the foot of the landin' arguin'
Said "Look like the man done pulled out all the lady's*
   dresser drawers"

Yes I walked out left the police on the landin' arguin'
Said "Look like the man done pulled out all the lady's*
   dresser drawers"

But he say "I got the letter to show the judge
The boy just tryin' to find
                    his Santa Claus"

(Oh yes)

—*Sonny Boy Williamson*

27. GOOD THING BLUES

1. Good things
My baby make good things come to my remind

Good things
My baby make good things come to my remind

Ev'ry time she throws her arms around me
I don't do a thing but act a clown

2.   Man y'know my baby went out last night and got*
         drunk
      Man that's somethin' I really can't stand
      She came home this mornin' kickin' up on the door
      "Doctor Ross I done found me another man

---

*line should continue but page prevents it from doing so.

Because he make good things"
My baby make good things come to my remind

'n ev'ry time she throws her arms around me
I don't do a thing but act a clown

3. Good things
My baby make good things come to my remind

Good things
My baby make good things come to my remind

You know when she throws her arms around me
I don't do a thing but act a clown
(Play the blues man)

4.　　　　Man you know my baby said she's goin' away for*
　　　　　　four or five months
　　　　She said "Doctor Ross I'll be back home soon
　　　　If I don't come back home Wednesday evenin'
　　　　You can look for me Thursday in the afternoon*
　　　　　　'cause you make good things"

My baby make good things come to my remind

Ev'ry time she throws her arms around me
I don't do a thing but act a clown

—Doctor Ross

28. NEW CRAWLIN' KING SNAKE

1.　　　　Well I crawled up to your window one morning
　　　　Crawled to your bed
　　　　I'm gonna make you take back

---

line should continue but page prevents it from doing so.

The words you have said
Because I'm your crawlin' king snake
You know I'm here to rule my den

Don't want nobody foolin' with you baby
I want to use you for my friend

2.   Well why don't you feed me baby
          Where I can get down low
          You don't feed me baby I'm gon'
          Crawl from your door
I'm your crawling king snake
You know I rule my den

I don't want nobody foolin' with you woman
I want to use you for my friend

3.   Well I crawled out on the grass this morning
          When the grass was high
          Expect to keep on crawlin'
          Till the day I die
I'm your crawlin' king snake
And you know I rule my den

I don't want nobody foolin' with you woman
I want to use you for my friend

4.   Well I crawled out on the grass baby
          And crawled up on your porch
          Ain't nothin' I want woman
          I'm just curled up out your door
I'm your crawlin' king snake
You know I rule my den

Don't want nobody foolin' with you
I want to use you for my friend

—Howlin' Wolf

29. MAN AROUND MY DOOR

1. There's a strange man
   Keeps on hangin' 'round my door

   There's a strange man
   Keeps on hangin' 'round my door

   I would let you in
   But my man would make you go

2. Go away from my window
   Don't set down on my doorstep

   Go away from my window
   Don't set down on my doorstep

   I don't need me no more lovin'
   My lover he just left

3. He's got two gold teeth
   Soft black curly hair

   He's got two gold teeth
   Soft black curly hair

   When he walk down the the street
   The sun shine bright everywhere

—Grace Brim

30. KATIE MAE

1. Yeah you know Katie Mae is a good girl
   Folks and she don't run around at night

   Yeah you know Katie Mae is a good girl
   Folks and she don't run around at night

Yeah you know you can bet your last dollar
Katie Mae will treat you right

2.   Yeah you know I try to give that woman
Everything in the world she need
That's why she don't do nothing but
Lay up in the bed and read you know she walks*
     just like
She got oil wells in her backyard

Yes you'll never hear that woman whoop and holler and cry
And talkin' 'bout these times bein' hard

3. You know some folks say she must be a Cadillac
But I say she must be a T-model Ford

Yeah you know some folks say she must be a Cadillac
But I say she must be a T-model Ford

Yeah you know she got the shape all right
But she can't carry no heavy load

4. I say goodbye goodbye poor Katie Mae
These are the last words that I got to say

I say goodbye goodbye poor Katie
These are the last words I got to say

Yes if I don't see you tomorrow
I hope I'll meet you early the next day

—*Lightnin' Hopkins*

31. TELL ME BABY

1. Tell me baby
What you want me to do

---

line should continue but page prevents it from doing so.

Tell me baby
What you want old Hogan to do

It ain't nothin' I like baby
Than spending my time with you

2. It's gettin' late baby
I hear the rooster's crowin' for day

It's gettin' late baby
I hear the rooster's crowin' for day

I want you to turn over woman
And hear what I have to say

3. The sun is rising
I see the shadow's in my face

The sun is rising
I see the shadow's in my face

When I leave here babe
Your other man gon' take my place

—Silas Hogan

32. HONEY BEE

1. Sail on
Sail on my little honey bee sail on

Sail on
Sail on my little honey bee sail on

You gonna keep on sailing
Till you lose your happy home

2. Sail on
   Sail on my little honey bee sail on

   Sail on
   Sail on my little honey bee sail on

   I don't mind you sailing
   But please don't sail so long
   (All right little honey bee
   Please have mercy)

3. I hear a lot of buzzing
   Sounds like my little honey bee

   I hear a lot of buzzing
   Sounds like my little honey bee

   She been all around the world making honey
   But now she is coming back home to me

                                    —*Muddy Waters*

33. HENRY'S SWING CLUB

1. (Yes boy
   I really know
   My mama didn't allow me to boogie woogie
   And I knowed that.
   One night I heard mama and papa talking.
   Papa said, "Mama,
   Let this child boogie woogie.
   It's in him
   And it's got to come out of him.")
   Papa say I could boogie woogie anyhow
   Hey
   Well I didn't care now
   He say I could boogie woogie anyhow

2. (One day I was walking down Hastings Street.
   That's when I first came to town.
   I didn't know nobody.
   I asked the man, said, "What town is this?"
   He said, "This is Detroit.
   Boy it really jumps here."
   Met a little chick, said, "Hey there!"
   I said, "Hey there, baby."
   I said, "Where you goin'?"
   "I want to go to Henry's Swing Club where I can jump*
        tonight.")
   She said "Let's go daddy
   I said daddy let's have a ball"

3. (When I got there that night,
   Boy the chick was in the groove.
   I reached in my coat, you know.
   I had just come to town, I didn't know all about the*
        rackets.
   She said, "Set down, oh set down." I said, "No, baby.")
   Said, "Let's boogie woogie awhile
   While the fun is goin' on"

4. (Yes I know.
   Boy that chick could boogie woogie, too.
   She start to boogie'n and susie-q'in', jitterbuggin', doing*
        everything.
   I didn't want to be the kind of a guy you know that
   That didn't know.
   I started 'round you know.
   After awhile I started jumpin'. Boy I was jumpin'.)
   Then I started jumpin'
   I been jumpin' ever since that day

                                        —*John Lee Hooker*

---

line should continue but page prevents it from doing so.

34. MISS LORETTA

1. Whoa Miss Loretta
   Where did you get all these good looking women from?

   Well well Miss Loretta lord will you please tell me baby
   Where did you get all these good looking women from?

   She said they come in here unexpected you know they was
   Blowed in here by a storm

2. I said, "Sugar mama sugar mama now
   Will you please come back to me?

   Sugar mama sugar mama
   Won't you please ma'am come back to me?

   Yes I say bring me my granulated sugar
   Oh lord and ease my misery"

3.   Yes Miss Loretta here's something I got to tell you
             I want you to do
             Long as you live I want you to keep these women
             'Round here with you I said Miss
   Please ma'am Miss Loretta
   Keep these womens here with you
   Cause I might be a sugar maker and I may make it just as
   Sweet as sugar can be

4.   Yeah you know I went to church last night
             I didn't get there on time
             They called on me to pray and I had prayin' on*
                 my mind thinking about Miss

   Loretta and the women
   Yes man they was on my mind

---

line should continue but page prevents it from doing so.

Yes I thought about how nice Miss Loretta was and how*
   the
Women treated me so nice and kind

—Lightnin' Hopkins

35. LONG WAY FROM TEXAS

1. I come all the way from Texas
   Just to shake glad hands with you

   I come all the way from Texas
   Just to shake glad hands with you

   Yes but when I seed in your smilin' face
   I didn't know just what to do

2. I ought to been knowing
   These things for a great long time

   I ought to been knowing
   These things for a great long time

   You know it take me for quite awhile
   'Fore I made it up in my mind
   (Got to play it a minute)

3. I'm gonna tell all my friends
   Just as soon as I go back home

   I'm gonna tell all my friends
   Just as soon as I go back home

   I know they all gonna get on and wonder
   What is I been waitin' on

—Lightnin' Hopkins

---

*line should continue but page prevents it from doing so.

36. SWEETEST WOMAN

1. Sweetest woman
   That I ever seen

   Sweetest woman
   That I ever seen

   You know the woman I'm lovin'
   Brought from New Orleans

2. Fix my breakfast
   Bring my meals to the bed

   Fix my breakfast
   Bring my meals to the bed

   When I'm tired and worried
   Rubs my achin' head

3. Never whiskey
   Never got her gin

   Never whiskey
   Never got her gin

   Said she hadn' a good man
   Lord in God knows when

4. Come on in
   Lay down cross my bed

   Come on in
   Lay down cross my bed

   I want to give you plenty lovin'
   Do your job up right

5. Don't need no money
   You don't need no job

   Don't need no money
   You don't need no job

You say you don't have to worry
'Bout this time's bein' hard

6. Sweetest woman
That I ever seen

Sweetest woman
That I ever seen

You know the woman I'm lovin'
Brought from New Orleans

7. Got me a home
Down on Rampart Street

Got me a home
Down on Rampart Street

When you see her downtown she's dressed up from her
Head to her feet

—*Joe Hill Louis*

37. SO SAD TO BE LONESOME

1. It's so sad to be lonesome
Too much unconvenient to be alone

You know it's so sad to be lonesome
But it's too much unconvenient to be alone

You know it makes a man feel
so good
When his baby's lyin' down in his arms

2. I received a letter from my baby
I received a telegram

I received a letter from my baby
And I received a telegram

Then the little girl called me long distance she wants to*
    know
Just where
            I am

3.   When you miss your baby
           You look around
           Can't see nothing but just
           Your shade on the ground
So sad to be lonesome
I know it's too much unconvenient to be alone

But I declare you feel good
When your baby come back home

4.   Met the Greyhound bus
           Met the train
           She wasn't on either one, I want to know
           What was to blame
So sad to be lonesome
Too much unconvenient to be alone

But it make you feel so good
When your baby come back home

                        —*Sonny Boy Williamson*

---

line should continue but page prevents it from doing so.

III

I Can't Do It All By Myself

"You got to help me baby,
I can't do it all by myself."

—*Sonny Boy Williamson, "Help Me" (transcription 40).*

38. IT'S YOUR LIFE

1.   Listen baby
          I want to tell you what's right
          You better stop goin' out in the alley
          Gettin' drunk ev'ry night
    But it's your life
    Your life you got to live

    Well if you keep goin' down there
    You're bound to get somebody killed

2.   I used to have a woman
          The cutest thing in town
          I couldn't keep her out of Tin Pan Alley
          Now she's six feet under ground
    But it's your life
    Yes it's your life you got to live

    Well if you keep goin' down there
    You're bound to get somebody killed

3.   Now you can ask anybody
          From miles around
          They'll tell you Tin Pan Alley's
          The roughest place in town but it's your life
    Yes it's your life you got to live

    Well if you keep goin' down there
    You're bound to get somebody killed

                                        —*Johnny Fuller*

39. TAKE IT EASY BABY

1. Take it easy baby
   You may live a long long time

Take it easy baby
You may live a long long time

But you and your fast way of goin'
Make me bound to lose my mind

2.   Well you drink your whiskey baby
        You drink your wine
        You go your way
        Babe and I'll go mine so won't you take it easy
You may live a long long time

But the way you goin'
People I'm bound to lose my mind

3.   Well you run all up and down the street
        Runnin' other women's men
        You better take it easy baby
        Take it easy while you can 'cause your time
Baby you know your time ain't long

You may call it stay
Baby but I call it gone

4. Bad women and bad whiskey
   Oh man 'bout to take me down

   Bad women and bad whiskey
   Oh man 'bout to take me down

   I wake up in the mornin'
   Feel like a country clown

5. Take it easy baby
   Mind the things I say

   Take it easy baby
   Take it easy and listen to what I have to say
   Well if you don't quit your fast way of goin'
   Baby you won't live half *a day*

—*Nat Terry*

40. HELP ME

1. You got to help me
   I can't do it all by myself

   You got to help me baby
   I can't do it all by myself

   You know if you don't help me darlin'
   I'll have to find myself somebody else

2.   I may have to wash
         I may have to sew
         I may have to cook
         I might mop the floor but you
   Help me baby

   You know if you don't help me darlin'
   I'll find myself somebody else

3.   When I walk
         You walk with me
         And when I talk
         You talk to me
   Oh baby
   I can't do it all by myself

   You know if you don't help me darlin' I'll have to
   Find myself somebody else
   (Help me help me darlin')

4. Bring my nightshirt
   Put on your morning gown

   Well bring me my nightshirt
   Put on your morning gown

   Darlin' I know we ain't sleepy
   But I just feel like lyin' down
   (Oh yeah help me)

—*Sonny Boy Williamson*

41. THIS OLD LIFE

1. This old life
   I just can't stand to live it no more

   This old life
   I just can't stand
                      to live it no more

   Baby you got to help me get myself straightened up right*
      now
   If you don't I am
                      gon' have to go

2. I'm askin you baby
   Please help me
                   just once more

   Askin' you baby
   I'm askin' you please help me once more

   Because I'm gonna get myself straightened all out right now
   So I won't go wrong
                      no more

3. Help me baby
   Help me darlin'
                   just once more

   If you help me get myself straightened out this time
   I won't go wrong no more

4. I done you wrong
   And I'm askin' you to forgive

   Darlin' I done you wrong
   And I'm askin' you to forgive

---

*line should continue but page prevents it from doing so.

If you just help me get myself straightened out

> this time

Darlin' I know just how you feel

> please help me darlin'

> —*Sonny Boy Williamson*

42. YOUR FUNERAL AND MY TRIAL

1.   Please come home to your daddy
        And explain yourself to me
        Because I and you is man and wife
        Tryin' to start a family
I'm beggin' you baby
Cut out that off-the-wall jive

If you can't treat me no better
It's got to be your funeral

> and my trial

2.   Well now when you first got together
        It was on one Friday night
        We spent two lovely hours together
        And the world knew it was all right
I'm just beggin' you baby
Please cut out
            that off-the-wall jive

You know you've got to treat me better
If you don't it's got to be your funeral and my trial
(Well all right)

3.   The good Lord made the world and ev'ry
        Thing was in it
        The way my baby love it's a
        Solid sender
        She can love to heal the sick
        And she can love to raise the dead

You might
                    think I'm jokin' but you better be-
          lieve what I said
I'm beggin' you baby
Cut out that off-the-wall jive

Is you got to treat me better
It's got to be your funeral and my trial

—Sonny Boy Williamson

43. BUILD A CAVE

1.   This world is in a tangle baby now
          Ever'body singin' a song
          They're fightin' 'cross the water baby ain't gonna
          Be here long I'm gonna build myself a cave
So I can move down on the ground

So when I go into the army darlin'
Won't be no reds around

2.   I got my questionnairy baby now
          I got my class card too
          Uncle Sam he wants me in the army baby now
          Now what's I'm gonna do I'm gonna build myself *
              a cave
So I can move down on the ground

So when I go into the army darlin'
Won't be no reds around

3.   I was layin' down in my bed baby now
          Drunk as I could be
          I was layin' there drunk

---

line should continue but page prevents it from doing so.

When Uncle Sam started in after me I'm gonna*
    build myself a cave
So I can move down on the ground

So when I go into the army darlin'
Won't be no reds around

4.   I was gonna go to the deep blue sea
       My baby began to cry
       She began to holler "Naw naw
       Bye bye bye" I'm gonna build myself a cave
So I can move down on the ground

So when I go to the army darlin'
Won't be no reds around

—Mr. Honey

44. WAR NEWS BLUES

1. You may turn your radio on soon in the mornin'
  Sad news ev'ry day

  You may turn your radio on soon in the mornin'
  Sad news ev'ry day

  Yes you know I got a warnin'
  Trouble is on its way

2. Poor children runnin' cryin' "Whoa mama
  Mama now what shall we do?"

  Poor children runnin' cryin' "Whoa mama
  Mama now what shall we do?"

  "Yes" she said "you had better pray children
  Same thing is happenin' to mama too"

---

line should continue but page prevents it from doing so.

3. I'm gonna dig me a hole this mornin'
   Dig it deep down in the ground

   I'm gonna dig me a hole this mornin'
   Dig it deep down in the ground

   So if it should happen to drop a bomb around somewhere
   I can't hear the echo when it sound

                                        —Lightnin' Hopkins

45. DON'T LOSE YOUR EYE

1. Don't lose your eye
   Man to spite your face

   I don't want you to
                       lose no eye
   Man to spite your face

   Because the people started snitchin' on you
   Can't hide
           at no place

2. If you do right
   The world is goin' to find you out

   If you a wrong-doing person
   The world gon' find you out

   You know you can't do wrong and get by
   Ain't no need of tryin'
                          to dodge that doubt

3. If I was you
   I'd play fair in anything I do

   If I was you
   I would play fair in anything I do

Anytime the people find out that you crooked man they*
    not gon'
Do nothin' in the world for you

4. My daddy taught me
Ever since I was a child

My daddy taught me
Ever since I was a child

Always treat your
                    neighbors right
Be fair with your
                friends likewise

—*Sonny Boy Williamson*

46. SCHOOL DAYS

1.   Said when I was a little boy my mother tried to
        Send me to school
        I didn't want to go 'cause ain't no
        Nobody's fool but I got school days
School days on my mind

Say it's way too late now baby
Ain't no need of me standing here cryin'

2.   Said I 'member one evening boys you know
        'Bout half past three
        I see the school kids that's what
        People worries me you know I got school days
School days on my mind

Says there's nothing for me to do now
But I'm just standing here cryin'

---

line should continue but page prevents it from doing so.

3.   Well I went down to the judge man
        To try to explain
        He give me a pencil I couldn't even
        Sign my name I got school days
School days on my mind

Says I'm just so late too late
Always standin' 'round cryin'

4.   I'm gon' tell all you kids
        While you're young
        You better go to school and
        Don't be dumb I got school days
School days on my mind

And I'm way too late now
Always standin' 'round cryin'

—Floyd Jones

47. STILL A FOOL

1. Well now there's two
  There's two trains runnin'
  Well they ain't never no goin' my way
  Well now one run at midnight and the other one
  Runnin' just 'fore day
  It's runnin' just 'fore day
  It's runnin' just 'fore day
  Oh lord
  Sure 'nough they is
  Oh well

2. Mm mm
  Ho ho ho
  Somebody help me ho with these blues
  Well now she's the one I'm lovin' she's the one

I do hate to lose
I do hate to lose
I do hate to lose
Oh lord
Sure 'nough I do
Oh well

3. I been crazy
   Yes I been a fool
   I been crazy oh all of my life
   Well I done fell in love with a
   With another man's wife
   With another man's wife
   With another man's wife
   Oh lord
   Sure 'nough I done
   Oh well

4. Lord
   She's so long and tall
   Till she weep like a willow tree
   Well now they say she's no good but she's all right
   She's all right with me
   She's all right she's all right
   She's all right she's all right

—Muddy Waters

48. MY FAULT

1. It's my own fault
   I don't blame you for treatin' me the way you do

   It's my own fault
   I don't blame you for treatin' me the way you do

When you was deep in love with me
At that time little girl I didn't love you

2.   You used to make your paycheck
       And then bring it all home to me
       You know I would go up on the corner
       Make every woman drunk I see that's my own fault
         Honey I don't blame you for treatin' me the way*
         you do

When you was deep in love with me
At that time little girl I didn't love you

3.   You know I used to take you out little girl
       And keep you weeks after weeks
       You were so scared to quit me little darlin'
       I may make a 'fore day creep that's my own fault*
       girl
       Honey I don't blame you for treatin' me the way*
       you do

When you was deep in love with me
At that time little girl I wouldn't be true
       (Tell her everything, man.)

—*Muddy Waters*

49. COFFEE BLUES

1. Mama got mad at papa 'cause he didn't bring no coffee*
   home

  Mama got mad at papa 'cause he didn't bring no coffee*
   home

---

line should continue but page prevents it from doing so.

She begin to wonder
What is going on wrong

2. Papa said "Mama I ain't mad with you
Now don't you get mad with me

Baby I ain't mad with you
Now don't you get mad with me"

3. Papa must have been teasing mama 'cause she said "I ain't*
mad with you"

Papa must have been teasing mama 'cause she said "I ain't*
mad with you"

She said "Everything's all right don't make no difference*
what you do"

(You know papa got good with mama somehow.)

4. And I was cryin' for bread
And yes I

Baby I was cryin' for bread
And these are the words I said

(Now look at mama. Just tryin' to shout.)

5. It was early one evening but papa came home late at night

It was early one evening but papa came home late at night

That's when mama was mad and her and papa began to*
fight

—*Lightnin' Hopkins*

---

line should continue but page prevents it from doing so.

IV

The Living Have Gone So High

"The living have gone so high,
Darlin' I don't know what to do."

—*Floyd Jones, "Stockyard Blues" (transcription 51).*

50. DEMOCRAT BLUES

1.   Well do you remember baby
          Nineteen and thirty-one
          That's when the Depression baby
          Just begun yes darlin'
    If you know what I'm talkin' 'bout

    Well the Democrats put you on your feet baby
    You had the nerve to throw them out

2.   You didn't have to plant no more cotton baby
          You didn't have to plow no more corn
          If a mule was runnin' away with the world baby
          You'd tell him to go 'head on yes darlin'
    If you know what I'm talkin' 'bout

    Well the Democrats put you on your feet baby
    You had the nerve to throw them out

3.   Well do you remember baby
          When the steel mill shut down
          You had to go to the country
          Thought you couldn't live in town yes darlin'
    If you know what I'm talkin' 'bout

    Well the Democrats put you on your feet baby
    You had the nerve to throw them out
    (Yeah man
    Play it a long time
    Nineteen fifty-six
    Beat 'em beat 'em)

4.   Well do you remember baby
          When your stomach was *awfully slack*
          Somebody help me
          Get them Democrats back yes darlin'

If you know what I'm talkin' 'bout

Well the Democrats put you on your feet baby
You had the nerve to throw them out

—*Bo Bo Jenkins*

51. STOCKYARD BLUES

1.   Well I left home this morning boys you know
        'Bout half-past nine
        I passed the stockyard you know the boys were still
        On the picket line you know I need your hundred*
            dollars
    You know I need your hundred dollars

    Well it's 'cause the living have gone so high
    Darlin' I don't know what to do

2.   Well I went down to the butcher man you know
        In the showcase I get my feet
        He says I got a four cent raise man
        On all of my meat you know I need your hundred*
            dollars
                            (Lad how do you do on*
            a bunch of dollars)
    You know I need to make a dollar

    Well it's 'cause the living have gone so high
    Darlin' I don't know what to do
    (Your turn Snook)

3.   Well I caught the streetcar this morning boys you*
            know
        'Bout half-past four

---

line should continue but page prevents it from doing so.

I give the man his 'leven cent he says
"Son it's two cent more" you know I need your*
    hundred dollars
You know I need to make a dollar

Well it's 'cause the living have gone so high
Darlin' I don't know what to do
(All right Moody)

—Floyd Jones

52. THINGS ARE SO SLOW

1.   I went to work this mornin'
      Was all set to start
      My boss walked up and told me
      Something break my heart things so slow
Don't think we need you any more

He told me things was so slow
Don't think we need you any more

2.   I had to tell my wife
      She didn't fuss
      Finance took the car
      We'll have to ride the bus things is so slow
Don't think we'll be ridin' any more

I told her things was so slow
Don't think we'll be ridin' any more

3.   I had a dream last night
      I was standing in a great long line
      A line like they had boys
      In nineteen twenty-nine things was so slow

line should continue but page prevents it from doing so.

Don't think I'll make it any more

I said now things is so slow
Don't think I'll make it any more

4.   In nineteen forty-four
       Ev'rything was going 'long strong
       I says ten years later boys
       And ev'rything's gone wrong things is so slow
Don't b'lieve I can make it any more

I said now things is so slow
Don't think I can make it any more

—J. B. Hutto

53. TOUGH TIMES

1.   Me and my baby was talkin'
       And what she said is true
       Said "Seems like times is getting tough
       Like they was in 'thirty-two
       You don't have no job
       Our bills is past due"
       Said now "Tell me baby
       What we gonna do?" tough times
Tough time is here once more

Now if you don't have no money peoples
You can't live happy no more

2.   I had a good job
       Workin' many long hours a week
       They had a big layoff
       And they got poor me
       I'm broke and disgusted
       In misery

        Can't find a part-time job
        Nothin' in my house to eat tough times
Tough time is here once more

Now if you don't have no money
You can't live happy no more
(Go on Eddie)

3.   I went down to the grocery store
        See if I could get a little more food on time
        The man said "Wait a minute
        See how do we stand"
        Say "I'm sorry to tell you
        You're too far behind" tough times
Tough time is here once more

Now if you don't have no money
Can't live happy no more

—John Brim

54. REPOSSESSION BLUES

1. Well I ain't got no money
   I'm gonna lose ever'thing I own

   Well I ain't got no money
   I'm gonna lose ever'thing I own

   Oh yeah they are comin' out in the morning
   They're gonna repossess my home

2. Well they done got my television
   Now they're comin' for my radio

   Yes they got my television
   Now they're comin' for my radio

Well they don't like the way I'm doing
They'll say I paid my bills too slow

3. Yes I paid twenty dollars down
I got myself a brand-new automobile

Yes I paid twenty dollars down
I got myself a brand-new baby blue Bel-Air

Well now the bank they done come out and got it
Yes and I
          got to walk ever'where

—*Lightnin' Leon*

55. EVERYBODY WANTS TO KNOW

1. (Hey, little brother! Did they get you?) (Umh humh.)*
   (They got me too. Now you know I'm mad.)

                    One thing I hate
                    They all
                              got me in a *huff*
                    Lay off my sister and my brother right*
          back and got my dad and mother
   Uh uh uh
   I got them layin' off blues

   Thinkin' about me and you
   What the President gonna do

2.   Taken all my money
                 To pay them tax I'm just
                 Givin' you peoples
                 The nat'ral facts

---

line should continue but page prevents it from doing so.

> Ev'rytime I look around I pay
> Tax tax tax you have
> Taken all my money and will not give me none*
>   back
Uh uh uh
I got them layin' off blues

Thinkin' about me and you
What's the President gonna do

3. > You rich people listen you better listen real deep
> If we poor peoples get so hungry we gonna take*
>   some food to eat
Uh uh uh
I got them layin' off blues

Thinkin' about me and you
What's the President gonna do

—J. B. Lenoir

56. CANDY KITCHEN

1. Well I don't work in no candy kitchen little girl
   God knows I don't sell no chewing gum

   I don't work in no candy kitchen little girl
   God knows I don't sell no chewing gum

   Yes but still I don't have to grab no pick 'n' shovel*
       woman and
   Roll from sun to sun

2. Yes I woke up this mornin'
   Man the rain fallin' on the ground

---

*line should continue but page prevents it from doing so.

Yes I woke up this mornin'
Boy the rain fallin' on the ground

Yes I had to go work for the W. P. and A. and boys you*
    know it's
Way over 'cross town

3. Yes these is awful things
   Yes to hear a Black man say

   Yes these is awful things
   To hear a Black man say

   Yes you know I done throwed my shovel away

   'cause I*

       don't have to
   Work on that W. P. and A.

—*Lightnin' Hopkins*

57. LIVING IN THE WHITEHOUSE

1. I'm livin' in the White House
   Just tryin' to help old Ike along

   Now I'm livin' in the White House
   Just tryin' to help old
                       Ike along

   And to try to make an amendment
   For things Harry left undone

2. I don't need no pilot to
   Chauffeur me in no jet

   I don't need no chauffeur to
   Chauffeur me in no jet

line should continue but page prevents it from doing so.

Because I'm kinda in a hurry
I'll have to ride space cadet

3. I want to live in paradise make
   Servants out of
                    kings and queens

   I want to live in paradise make
   Servants out of kings and queens

   Now don't shake me please darlin'
   This is one time I want to finish my dream

—*Johnny Shines*

58. STRIKE BLUES

1. Oh lord oh lord baby
   What in the world's gonna become of me?

   I don't know don't know baby
                              lord lord lord
   What in the world's gonna become of me

   These hard times hard times baby
   'Bout to get the best of me

2.   (You know poor Chrysler God knows been on
            For ninety days already
            But it's one thing now people)
            Lord I sure can't understand
   I said oh
   What in the world's gonna become of me?

   If this doggone strike won't come over people
   God knows my life can't last me long

3.   (I go to the welfare
            Here's what the welfare said

"Looka here now man
One cup of beans
                    and one can of tripe")
I said no
God knows that will never do

If poor Chrysler soon won't end the strike God knows*
    God knows
I don't know what I'm gonna do

—*John Lee Hooker*

*line should continue but page prevents it from doing so.

V

I've Been Mistreated

"I've been mistreated;
You know just what I'm talkin' about."

—*Eddie Boyd, "Five Long Years" (transcription 77).*

59. HALF A STRANGER

1. I met a half a stranger one day boys
                                      one day boys
   I tried to sway
               her to be my wife

   She cut my pleasure in two
   Same as she had
                   a pocket knife
                   a pocket knife

2. I'm goin tell you boys and girls
   Tell you
           what you mustn't do
           you mustn't do

   Oh oh Lord oh Lord
                   mmmmmmmmmmmmmmm
   Whoa boys what you mustn't do

   When it comes to marryin'
   You better speak once
                   and think twice
                   and think twice

3. The little girl I married
   She 'bout to drive my life away
                               my life away

   I made a mistake in life
   And I never—oh
               do that again

4. Mmmmmmmmmm mm mmMM Mmmmmm mmMMmmm*
      mmmm
   I made a mistake in life
   I'll never do that again

                              —*John Lee Hooker*

---

line should continue but page prevents it from doing so.

60. LONESOME HOME

1. Ain't it lonesome ain't it lonesome
   Sittin' in your home alone

   Ain't it lonesome ain't it lonesome
   Sittin' in your home alone

   Yes you know when your wife done quit your Black self
   And the girl you love is gone

2.   Yeah you know she kinda like Katie Mae
       I give her ev'rything in the world she needs
       That's why she don't do nothin' man but
       Lay up in the bed and read and you know she's
   Kinda like Katie Mae
   Boy I give that woman ev'rything in the world she needs

   Yes that's why you know she don't do nothin' man
   Lay up in the bed and read

3.   Yes you know I bought her a radio
       I even bought her a 'lectric fan
       She said "Sam I'm gon' lay here and read and God*
           knows I won't have no other man" that made*
           me feel so good
   Till I don't know what to do

   Yes darlin' ev'ry dollar poor Sam makes you know
   He got to bring it back home to you
   (Got to play it out right here)

4.   Still I say can't a woman act funny I'm talkin about
       When she got another man
       You know she won't look straight at you boy she*
           always raisin' sand can't a

---

line should continue but page prevents it from doing so.

Woman act funny
Boy when she got another man

Yes you know she won't look straight at you
Then she's always raisin' sand

—*Lightnin' Hopkins*

61. THAT AIN'T RIGHT

1.   Now I give my baby the best
          Best of ev'rything she wants
          Yet and still she cheatin' on me
          Won't never stay at home
    That ain't right
    Baby treatin' me the way you do

    You know I love you darlin'
    That's why I put up
                    with the things you do

2.   Now you tell me you go to the movies
          But don't stay open all night long
          Yet you never come home baby
          Until the break of dawn
    That ain't right
    Baby
            treatin' me way you do

    You know I loves you baby
    That's why I put up
                    with the things you do

3.   Now you goin' when you get ready
          Come home when you please
          Most of the time you was very loaded
          And wobblin' in your knees that ain't right

Baby
     treat me way you do

You know I love you darlin'
That's why I put up with the
       things you do

         —*John Brim*

62. SHORT HAIRED WOMAN

1. I don't want no woman
If her hair ain't no longer'n mine

I don't want no woman
If her hair ain't no longer'n mine

Yes you know she ain't good for nothin' but trouble
That's keep you buyin' rats all the time

2.   Yes you know I carried my wife to the hairdresser
And this what the hairdresser said
She said "Sam I can't straighten your woman's*
    hair but
God knows I can treat her head" I told her "No
If her hair ain't no longer'n mine"

Yes you know she ain't good for nothin' but trouble
That keep you buyin' rats all the time

3.   Yes I got on the good side of my woman
I told her "Darlin' let's go have some fun"
I went to make a swing out but a rat fell from her*
    head like

---

line should continue but page prevents it from doing so.

One from a burning barn you know I don't
Want no woman
If her hair ain't no longer'n mine

Yes you know she ain't good for nothin' but trouble
That keep you buyin' rats all the time

4.   Yes you know I woke up this mornin' people you*
          know poor Sam
        He woke up 'bout the break of day
        I even found the rat on the pillow
        Where she used to lay you know I don't
Want no woman
If her hair ain't no longer'n mine

Yes you know she ain't good for nothin' but trouble
That keep you buyin' rats all the time

—*Lightnin' Hopkins*

63. PEPPER HEAD WOMAN

1. I got a pepper-headed woman
   Boys and her hair ain't very long

   I got a pepper-headed woman
   Boys her hair ain't very long

   Looks like a *pan of Turkish paint brand*
   Man they smeared it on

2.   Yeah you know she woke me up soon one mornin'
        Say "Daddy let's go out and pick some figs"
        You know I looked at that woman's hair it was so*

---

line should continue but page prevents it from doing so.

short till it couldn't even hold her wig 'cause*
she's a
Pepper-headed woman
Boys and her hair ain't very long

Looks like a *pan of Turkish paint brand*
Man they smeared it on
(I got to beat it out right there a little bit now)

3.   Yes she went down to the hairdresser
        For the hairdresser to straighten her hair
        She say "Miss I'll have to grease your head*
            because there
        Ain't no hair up there" 'cause she's a
Pepper-headed woman
Boys her hair ain't very long

Look like a *pan of Turkish paint brand*
Man they smeared it on

—*Square Walton*

64. GIVE ME BACK THAT WIG

1. Give me back that wig I bought you baby
   Darlin' let your doggone head go bald

   Give me back that wig I bought you baby
   Darlin' let your doggone head go bald

   Yes I come to find out this mornin' (God bless your heart)
   Baby you don't need no hair at all

2.   Yeah you know I bought you a wig
        I say "We're goin' out and have some fun"

---

*line should continue but page prevents it from doing so.

I looked around for you baby and what did I face a
Great big gun give me back that
Wig I bought you woman please ma'am
Let your doggone head go bald

Yes you know I done come to find out
You don't need no hair at all

3. Yeah you know my Mama she done told me
Told me just what a woman'd do

Yeah you know my mama she told me
Told me just what a woman'd do

Yes "If she can't get a wig from the store she'll come*
    'round and try to
Buy one of them things from you"

—*Lightnin' Hopkins*

65. MONEY TAKING WOMAN

1.   Can't understand holding up my hand
            Me and my baby's gonna raise some sand
    She's a money takin' woman
    She's a money takin' woman
    She's a money takin' woman and she takes it all the time

2.   You know she takes my money
            She calls me Jack
            She holds her hands out for it she never give it*
                back
    She is a money takin' woman
            (That's right boy that's my babe)

---

*line should continue but page prevents it from doing so.

She is a money takin' woman
She's a money takin' woman and she takes it all the time
(I got it boy)

3.   Now here we stand
            Toe to toe
            I'm gon' give you this money ain't gon' give you*
                no more
You's a money takin' woman
You's a money takin' woman
You's a money takin' woman and you takes it all the time

4.   Bye bye baby and I'm leaving you now
            Bye bye baby I don't want you nohow
You's a money takin' woman
You's a money takin' woman
You's a money takin' woman and you takes it all the time

5.   You said you give me your money 'cause you give*
                me your'n
            Sold my house and all I own
You's a money takin' mama
You's a money takin' woman
You's a money takin' woman and you takes it all the time

—Johnny Young

66. BIG TOWN PLAYBOY

1.   My baby told me last night
            To find yourself a job
            I told her Chicago was okay but these time was too
            Doggone hard she say "You're too lazy"

---

line should continue but page prevents it from doing so.

That's one thing my baby don't enjoy

I told her "Ever'thing is okay baby"
But I ain't nothin' but a big town playboy

2.　　　　She say "You walk the streets all day
　　　　You won't come home at night
　　　　Now you know little Johnny that you ain't
　　　　Treat' me right 'cause you're too lazy"
That's one thing my baby don't enjoy

She say "Ever'thing's okay little Johnny
But you ain't nothin' but a big town playboy"
(Lay me some racket boy lay me some racket)

3.　　　　She say "You go sharp ev'ry day
　　　　That's one thing the people can't understand
　　　　Now if you don't get yourself a job Johnny I'm*
　　　　　　gonna get me a
　　　　Brand new man 'cause you're too lazy"
That's one thing my baby don't enjoy

She say "Ev'rything is okay little Johnny
You ain't nothin' but a big town playboy"

—*Little Johnny Jones*

67. CHICAGO BLUES

1. Just from San Antonio Texas
Tryin' to work my way back home

Just from San Antonio Texas
Tryin' to work my way back home

---

line should continue but page prevents it from doing so.

Look like some of these Chicago womens
Tryin' to make me do somethin' wrong

2. You'd better speak to your lady
She's just winked her eye at me

You'd better speak to your lady
She's just winked her eye at me

I been drinkin' Joe Louis whiskey
I'm just as treach'rous as I can be
(Howl now)

3. Boys if you wants your womens
You better keep them in a line

Mens if you wants your women
You better keep them in a line

'Cause you know the one I've got
She keeps me worried all the time

—*Little Johnny Jones*

68. BLACK MAN BLUES

1. Tell me
God give a Black man
Most anything he do

Tell me
God give a Black man
Most anything he do

Well if that's the case I'm gonna
Kill this woman now I'm gonna
Drop down on the bed

2. Soon this mornin'
   Woman come walkin'
   That woman come
                        walkin in

   Yes
        soon this mornin'

   Woman come walk
                    walkin' in

   Yes I was
            layin' there thinkin' tryin' to
                                    make it up
                                            in my*

      mind

   Well and if I
               kill this woman
                            get down
                                   on her knees

3. Yes yes you know
                    know for certain
   Know she ain't doin' me right

   Yes house ain't never clean
   My supper it ain't never done

   Yes house ain't clean
   Supper it ain't never done

4. Yeah
            Got so mad this mornin'
            Broke to the wall right through there
            Grabbed my shotgun I started to
            Mow that woman down

---

*line should continue but page prevents it from doing so.

Yeah broke to the wall start to
       Mow that woman down
       Mow that woman down

Well now
       conscience told me Lord to
'Low her one more chance

                      —*John Lee Hooker*

69. WHEN THE SUN IS SHINING

1. (Oh boy I done spent all my money
   You know I ain't got no place to go
   Listen to me I want to tell you why)

   Baby when the sun was shining
   Lord that I could not go
   I done spent all my money
   Babe ain't got no more
   When the sun is shining
   I done throwed all my money away

   Well it caused me to beat now
   Poor little widow today

2. Well now I had a good woman
   Yes I was livin' in town
   I spent all that woman's money
   Boy and that girl she put me down when the sun was*
      shining
   I done throwed all my money away

   Well it caused me to beat now
   Poor little widow today

---

line should continue but page prevents it from doing so.

3. Well now I'm gon' tell all you men
   Gonna take my advice
   Don't go out and get drunk man
   Come home mistreat your wife when the sun is shining
   You done throwed all your money away

   Well it caused me to beat now
   Poor little widow today

                                          —L. C. Green

70. PLAYING THE RACES

1. I don't want no woman
   Plays the races all the time

   I don't want no woman
   Plays the races all the time

   You know she ain't good for nothin'
   Keep you broke most all the time

2. Dreamed a number last night
                        (yes yes yes)
   And my baby she did the same

   Dreamed a number last night
   And my baby did the same

   My baby got up this mornin'
   And she played it just the same
   (Yes man)

3. I come home ev'ry Friday
   Throws my check down on the bed

   I come home ev'ry Friday
   Throws my check down on the bed

My baby takes all of my money
Put it down on five
                  sixty-two
(Yes yes)

4. I don't want no woman
Play the races all the time

—John Lee Hooker

71. LONG DISTANCE CALL

1. You said you love me darlin'
Please call me on the phone sometime

You said you love me darlin'
Please call me on the phone sometime

When I hear your voice
Ease my worried mind

2. One of these days
I'm gon' show you how nice a man can be

One of these days
I'm gon' show you just how nice a man can be

I'm gon' buy you a brand new Cadillac
If you'll only speak some good words about me

3. Hear my phone ringing
Sound like a long distance call

Hear my phone keep ringing
Sound like a long distance call

When I picked up my receiver
The party said "Another mule kickin' in your stall"

—Muddy Waters

72. BAD WOMAN BLUES

1. I know it wasn't nothing but the devil
   Make my baby change her ways

   I know it wasn't nothing but the devil
   Made my baby change her ways

   My baby done got to be a notoriety woman
   You know and she ain't no earthly good

2.   Now you know my mm-baby she didn't go no*
              place
           But to church and the Sunday School
           But now she run around in ev'ry notoriety joint in*
              town
           And have ev'ry man she meet
   But I know it wasn't nothing but the devil
   Made my baby change her ways

   My babe done got to be a notoriety woman
   You know and she ain't no earthly good

3.   Now you know my mm-baby she can't read
           My baby can't even write
           My baby don't try to jive me
           She know I know what she's puttin' down
   But I know it wasn't nothing but the devil
   Made my baby change her ways

   My babe done got to be a notoriety woman
   You know and she ain't no earthly good

4.   Now you know my mm-baby I told her "I love*
              you"
           Want her to stop her runnin' 'round

---

line should continue but page prevents it from doing so.

She say "Ed if you don't like the way I'm doin'
You get you somebody else"
But I know it wasn't nothing but the devil
Made my baby change her ways

My babe done got to be a notoriety woman
You know she ain't no earthly good

—*Eddie Burns*

73. DON'T START ME TO TALKIN'

1.   Well I'm
        Goin' down to Rosie's
        Stop at Fannie Mae's
        Gon' tell Fannie what I heard
        Her boyfriend say don't
        Start me to talkin'
I'll tell ev'rything I know

I'm gon' break up this signifyin'
'Cause somebody's got to go

2.   Jack give his wife two dollars go downtown
        And get some market
        Gets out on the streets
        Old George stopped her
        He knocked her down
        And blackened her eye
        She gets back home
        Tells her husband a lie don't
        Start me to talkin'
I'll tell ev'rything I know

I'm gon' break up this signifyin'
Somebody's got to go

3.   She borrowed some money
            Go to the beauty shop
            She honked his horn
            She begin to stop
            Said "Take me baby
            Around the block
            I'm goin' to the beauty shop where I can
            Get my hair a sock" don't
            Start me to talkin'
       I'll tell ev'rything I know

       Well to break up this signifyin'
       Whoa somebody's got to go

                              —*Sonny Boy Williamson*

74. YOU CAN'T MAKE THE GRADE

1.   When your woman get funny
            When you start to gettin' old
            Now this is a story
            And it's never been told
       Too late old man
       All your debt must be paid

       Yeah your race is run
       You really can't make the grade

2.   Now that you worked like a ox
            You come home tired as a mule
            You get sixty years old
            Before you know it you's a fool
       Too late old man
       All your debts must be paid

       Yeah your race is run
       You really can't make the grade

3.   At midnight she shake you
           She know that's just a joke
           She know you goin' in the mornin'
           Before she gets you woke
  Too late old man
  All your debts must be paid

  Yeah your race is run
  You really can't make the grade

4.   Monday you feel like playin'
           She don't know your game
           Tuesday mornin' come
           Things about the same
           Wednesday she false accuse you
           Of some other chick
           Thursday when you touch her
           She says she's kinda sick
           Friday when you come she grab you
           She kiss you on the cheek
           She know she gon' to have enough money
           To last all the week
  Too bad old man
  All your debts must be paid

  Yeah your race is run
  You really can't make the grade

—*James "Beale Street" Clark*

75. IN MY YOUNGER DAYS

1. In my younger days
   I wished I knowed then like I know now

   In my younger days
   I wished I knowed then like I know now

I wouldn't be standin' 'round here beggin'
For this little
                    woman to let me in her house

2. Back in those days
   I wished I'd knowed then like I know now

   Back in those days
   I wished I'd knowed then like I know now

   The money I was throwin' away
   I could have saved it and bought my
                                        own house
   (And I'd've had a home)

3. In my younger days
   I wish I knowed then like I know now

   Well in my younger days
   I wished I
            knowed then like
                            I knowed now

   I wouldn't be standin' 'round beggin' this
   Woman
         to let me
                   in her house

                              —*Sonny Boy Williamson*

76. HOODOO HOODOO

1.   Knowling I wonder what's the matter with the times
          It seems like ev'rything have changed
          It seems like this woman that I have been lovin'*
          have

---

line should continue but page prevents it from doing so.

Have found some other man I hold up my hand
I'm just tryin' to get my baby to understand

See if my baby don't love me no more
Or because somebody have hoodooed the hoodoo man

2.   Well now and I'm gon' down in Louisiana
        And buy me another mojo hand
        All because I've got to break up my baby
        From lovin' this other man now I hold up my hand
I'm just tryin' to make my baby understand

'Cause my baby don't love me no more
She say "Somebody have hoodooed the hoodoo man"
(Well all right John
Yeah now Lacey)

3.   I used to have a way with womens
        Make plenty money and ev'rything
        But my woman don't love me no more
        She said "Somebody have hoodooed the hoodoo*
            man" now I just hold up my hand
I'm just tryin' to get my baby to understand

'Cause my baby don't love me no more
'Cause she say "Somebody have hoodooed the hoodoo man"

4.   Well now and goodbye baby
        Someday I'll see you soon
        I've got somethin' to tell you baby
        "Somebody else can have your room" and I hold*
            up my hand
I'm just tryin' to get my baby to understand

Yeah my baby don't love me no more
She say "Somebody have hoodooed the hoodoo man"

—*John Lee Williamson*

*line should continue but page prevents it from doing so.

77. FIVE LONG YEARS

1. If you ever been mistreated
   You know just what I'm talkin' about

   Well if you ever been mistreated
   You know just what I'm talkin' about

   I worked five long years for one woman
   She had the nerve to put me out

2.   I got a job in a steel mill
          A-truckin' steel like a slave
          For five long years ev'ry Friday I went straight*
             home with all my pay if you've
   Ever been mistreated
                 uh you know just what I'm talkin'*
     about

   I worked five long years for one woman
   She had the nerve to put me out

3.   I had a death in my family
          She wouldn't give me a helping hand
          I borrowed two or three dollars from the woman*
             she said "Hurry up and pay it back old man" if*
             you've
   Ever been mistreated
   Uh you know what I'm talkin' about

   I worked five long years for one woman
   She had the nerve to put me out

4.   I finally learned a lesson
          I should have known a long time ago

---

*line should continue but page prevents it from doing so.

The next woman I marry has got to work and*
    bring me some dough
I've been mistreated
You know just what I'm talkin' about

I worked five long years for one woman
She had the nerve to put me out

                            —*Eddie Boyd*

78. MAMA'S BABY CHILD

1. I was borned on the *levee*
   I'm my mama's baby child

   I was borned on the levee
   I'm my mama's baby child

   Yes you know it ain't but one thing I hate some women*
     have
   Made mama's baby wild

2. Yes if I'd have listened
   Yes to what my mama said

   If I'd have listened
   Yes to what my mama said

   Yes you know I wouldn't be here this evenin' I'm talkin'*
     about
   With a hung-down head

3. Yes you know I'm goin' back home to mama
   Fall down on my mama's knee

---

*line should continue but page prevents it from doing so.

I'm goin' back home to mama
Fall down on my mama's knee

Yes you know I'm gonna ask my mama will she
Please ma'am pray for me

—Lightnin' Hopkins

79. WHAT WRONG HAVE I DONE

1. Sometimes I begin wonderin' baby
   What wrong have I done

   Sometimes I begin wonderin' baby
   Mama what wrong have I done

   Look like all the woman I love, man
   You mistreats me just for fun

2. I got the blues so bad baby
   They hurt my feet to walk

   I got the blues so bad baby
   They hurt my feet to walk

   It done settled on my brains
   You know it hurt my poor tongue to talk

3. I said bye bye baby
   Mama won't you please come home to me

   I said please mama
   Baby won't you please come home to me

   You know I'm blue and disgusted
   And *worried* as a man can be
   (Yeah you know I'm gonna play one. You know what I*
       mean.)

---

line should continue but page prevents it from doing so.

4. I got the blues so bad baby
   I don't now what in the world I'm gonna do

   I got the blues so bad baby   .
   I don't know what in the world I'm gonna do

   I'm blue and disgusted baby
   And I'm worried over you

                                        —*Country Slim*

80. BAD LOVER BLUES

1. I've got a real bad lover
   I've got a real bad lover blues

   I've got a real bad lover
   I've got a real bad lover blues

   Yes if my baby don't make a change
   I know she going to have them too

2.   Here's what my baby done
          She snapped a pistol in my face
          "Baby Boy if you ain't careful I'm gonna send you*
             to your grave"
   Ain't that a real bad lover
   Ain't that a real bad lover blues

   Yes if my baby don't make a change
   I know she going to have them too

3.   Now you come to me in the winter
          You stay with me until spring
          No sooner times get better that's when you find*
             yourself a man

---

line should continue but page prevents it from doing so.

Ain't that a real bad lover
Ain't that a real bad lover blues

Yes if my baby don't make a change
I know she going to have them too
(Yes, I know what you mean.)

4.   Just because he's got a Cadillac with that*
        hydromatic drive
       You don't ask him for no money all you want to*
        do is ride
Ain't that a real bad lover
Ain't that a real bad lover blues

Yes if my baby don't make a change
I know she going to have them too

5.   Well I know you don't love me baby
       From the way you dog me 'round
       You just *keepin' me company baby*
       's got to the place I'm just your clown
Ain't that a real bad lover
Ain't that a real bad lover blues

Yes if my baby don't make a change
I know she going to have them too

—*Baby Boy Warren*

81. DON'T LAUGH AT ME

1. Don't laugh at me
Baby please don't make fun of me

Don't laugh at me
Baby don't make fun of me

---

line should continue but page prevents it from doing so.

Bear it in mind
There's time for everything

2. I know you got fine clothes
That's why you laughs at me

I know you got fine clothes
That's why you laughin' at me

Bear it in mind baby
There's a time for everything

3. Please don't laugh at me
Please don't laugh at me

Please don't laugh at me
Please don't laugh at me

I know I'm not good-lookin' baby
And I know I didn't make myself

4. I know you got a fine car baby
You can ride and enjoy yourself

I know you got a fine car baby
You can ride and enjoy yourself

I like to see you enjoy yourself baby
But please don't laugh at me

5. Didn't make myself baby
Didn't make myself

Didn't make myself baby
No I didn't make myself

Bear it in mind
There's a time for everything

—Howlin' Wolf

82. STREET LOAFIN' WOMAN

1.   Well I believe in being friends
            To all my neighborhood
            But I got a doggin' little woman she just
            Don't mean me no good because she don't want to
Do nothin'
Loaf around in the street

I'm gonna let her go because she
Ain't no good to me

2.   Now I go to work in the morning
            I have to leave home soon
            Before I can get outdoors
            Some man's been comin' in my room because that*
                woman
Don't do nothin'
Loaf around all in the street

I'm gonna let her go
                        because she
Ain't no good to me

3.   Now let me tell you something now Jay
            What that woman'll do
            I done bring her my paycheck she'll call
            Me her little fool because she don't
Want to do nothin'
Loaf around all in the street

I'm gonna let her go
She ain't no good to me
            (Watch out there Nicholson. Beat out some blues*
    now.

---

*line should continue but page prevents it from doing so.

Yes hard to have a woman
Don't mean you no good
Love every man she sees.)

4.   Now when I come home in the evenin'
I get there about four
If I don't find a man in my house
I'll find a big pallet on my floor because she don't
Want to do nothin'
Loaf around all in the street

Lord I'm gonna let her go because she
Ain't no good to me

— *Jimmy McCracklin*

83. GYPSY WOMAN

1. You know the gypsy woman told me
That you your mother's bad-luck child

You know the gypsy woman told me
That you your mother's bad-luck child

Well you're havin' a good time now
But that'll be trouble after while

2.   Well you know I went to a gypsy woman
To have my fortune told
She say "You better go back home son and peep*
through your
Your key hole" you know the gypsy woman told*
me

---

line should continue but page prevents it from doing so.

That you your mother's bad-luck child

Well you're having a good time now
But that'll be trouble after while

3.   Well now you know I went back home
            I took the gypsy woman as she said
            I peeped through my keyhole and there was*
                another man layin'
            In my bed you know the gypsy woman told me
That you your mother's bad luck child

Well you're having a good time now
But that'll be trouble after while

— *Muddy Waters*

84. PEACE BREAKING PEOPLE

1. Who—oo—oo—oo—oo—oo
   Who been telling you

   Who—oo—oo—oo—oo
   Who been telling you

   Everything I say
   Every little thing I do

2. Now I know why
   We can't get along no more

   I know why
   We can't get along no more

   You got someone watchin' me
   Everywhere I go

---

line should continue but page prevents it from doing so.

3. Nothing that she seen
   Something the poor girl heard

   Nothing that she seen
   Something the poor girl heard

   She left me this morning
   She didn't even say a word

4. These peace-breaking people
   Made you turn your back on me

   These peace-breaking people
   Made you turn your back on me

   One day you gon' be sorry
   You just wait and see

—Lil' Son Jackson

85. NERVY WOMAN BLUES

1. Somebody must have give my baby a pistol
   She got nerve like Jesse James

   Somebody must have give my baby a pistol
   She got nerve like Jesse James

   She'll get even and angry after hours
   And search the whole town to find her man

2. She left my layin' down in my bedroom
   "I might be back between now and day"

   She left me layin' down in my bedroom
   "Might be back between now and day"

   "Aw but if I find out what I'm thinkin'
   You'll have to hustle up a fine to pay"

3. I believe this woman have been a murderer
   She argues and fights all in her dreams

   I do believe she killed somebody
   She argues and fights all in her dreams

   Every morning I ask her what is the matter
   And she roll her eyes and look so mean

4. One morning she come home looking guilty
   I asked the girl where did she go

   Yes she come home looking guilty
   I asked the girl where did she go

   Said "Robert you ought to be prosecuted
   For asking a question you don't want to know"

   (I know what I'm gon' do
   I'm gonna let that woman go)

   —*Baby Boy Warren*

VI

I'm Gonna Have To Let Her Go

"Yes you know she's a sweet little girl,
But I'm gonna have to let her go."

    —*L. C. Williams, "Hole in the Wall" (transcription 94).*

86. FATTENING FROGS FOR SNAKES

1. It took me a long time
   To find out my mistake

   It took me a long time
   Long time to find out
                 my mistake
   (It sure did man)
   But I'll bet you my bottom dollar
   I'm not fattenin' no more
                 frogs for snakes

2. I found out my downfall
   Back in nineteen and thirty-eight
   (I started to checkin')
   I found out my downfall
   From nineteen and thirty-eight

   I'm tellin' all my friends I'm not
   Fattenin' no more
                 frogs for snakes
   (All right now)

3. Here it is nineteen and
                 fifty-seven
   I got to correct all of my mistakes

   Whoa man
            nineteen and fifty-seven I got to
   Correct all of my mistakes

   I'm tellin' my friends includin' my wife
                 and ev'rybody else
   I'm not fattenin' no more frogs for snakes

—*Sonny Boy Williamson*

87. SMOKE STACK LIGHTNIN'

1. O-oh smokestack lightnin'
   Shinin'
   Just like gold
   Huh don't you hear me cryin'
   Whoo — oo
   Whoo — oo
   Whoo — oo

2. We-ell tell me baby
   What's the
   Matter here
   Huh don't you hear me cryin' here
   Whoo — oo — oo
   Whoo — oo — oo — oo
   Whoo — oo

3. We-ell tell me baby
   Where did you
   Stay last night
   Oh don't you hear me cryin'
   Whee — oo
   Whee — oo — oo
   Whee — oo

4. We-ell stop your train
   Let a
   Poor boy ride
   Why don't you hear me cryin'
   Whoo — oo
   Whoo — oo — oo — oo
   Whoo — oo

5. We-ell fare you well
   Never see
   You no more

Oh don't you hear me cryin'
Whee — oo
Whee — oo — oo — oo
Whee — oo

6. O-oh who been here baby since
Uh I been gone
Little bitty boy
A derby on
Whee — oo
Whee — oo — oo — oo
Whee — oo

—Howlin' Wolf

88. LOCKED OUT BOOGIE

1. I went home last night my baby she wouldn't let me in
   I went home last night my baby wouldn't let me in
   She say go back to the North Side back to that old _____

2. I said uh "Please baby please don't let me go
   Please now baby please don't let me go
   All the time you were loving me baby you were loving*
     Mister So-and-so"
   (All right Bob)

3. I don't play the dozens cousin I can't stand the tens
   Don't play the dozens I
                          can't even stand the tens
   When you start 'em baby please don't deal me in

4. When a man ain't got no money the womens don't hang*
     around

---

line should continue but page prevents it from doing so.

When a man ain't got no money the womens don't want*
　　to hang around
But when a man got plenty of money you're the sweetest*
　　man in town

5. Fare you well baby I ain't got no more to say
　　Said "Fare you well baby I ain't got no more to say
　　Take Mister So-and-so let him come on and have his way"

—Leroy Foster

89. MISTREATED BLUES

1. I been mistreated so long
　　Babe it seems like my time ain't long

　　I been mistreated so long
　　Babe it seems like my time ain't long

　　Yeah you know if that woman don't come back this time
　　You can bet your last dollar the poor girl is dead and gone

2. Now I'm gonna carry my old shotgun
　　B'lieve I'll take along my forty-four

　　Now I'm gonna carry my old shotgun
　　B'lieve I'll take along my old forty-four

　　'Cause honey you done dogged me long enough
　　I declare you won't dog me no more

3. Ever since I been in love with you
　　Wolf's been hollerin' all in my door

　　Ever since I been in love with you
　　Say the wolf's been hollerin' all in my door

---

line should continue but page prevents it from doing so.

Yeah this is your last time now baby
Swear you won't dog me no more

4. Now goodbye baby
I declare I'm goin' on down the line

Yes bye bye baby
Honey I declare I'm goin' on down the line

Yes you can have your troubles in this world
Babe I declare I'll have mine

—*Buddy Chiles*

90. MOONSHINE BLUES

1. My baby love moonshine
And she drinks it all the time

My baby love moonshine
And she drinks it all the time

Well if she don't stop drinkin' muddy water
She's got to lose her worried mind
(I know what you mean son)

2. I can't see why my whiskey headed woman
Don't treat me good some time

Don't see why my whiskey head woman
Don't treat me good some time

Well I know the reason she don't love me
She got some other man on her mind

3. I may be here tomorrow
Next day I may be gone

May be here tomorrow
Next day I may be gone

I'm gon' find me some high brownskin
That's gon' make me feel good sometime
(Take it man)
Ooooh
        what's wrong
She just don't want to treat me right *now boys*)

—*Little Walter*

91. DOG ME AROUND

1. How many more years
   Have I got to let you dog me around

   How many more years
   Have I got to let you dog me around

   I'd just as soon rather be dead
   Sleepin' way down in the ground

2. If I treat you right
   You would believe what I've said

   If I treat you right
   You would believe what I've said

   You think I'm halfway crazy
   You think I ought to let you have your way

3. I'm goin' upstairs
   I'm gon' bring back down my clothes

   I'm goin' upstairs
   I'm gon' bring back down my clothes

   If anybody asks about me
   Just tell 'em I walked outdoors

—*Howlin' Wolf*

92. LUDELLA

1.   Now Ludella you know I even paid your house rent
            I got you ev'rything you need
            Now Ludella you done start' some side stuff baby
            You're runnin' 'round on me but Ludella Ludella
   Baby don't you hear me callin' you

   Now you know I've did all in the world I could Ludella
   Baby just tryin' to get along with you
   (Ride baby ride
   Give me the blues)

2.   Now and I says goodbye Ludella babe
            I declare I'm through with you
            You can keep on runnin' 'round woman I don't
            Care what in the world you do but Ludella Ludella
   Baby don't you hear me callin' you

   Now I've did ev'rything in this world
   Baby and I can't get along with you

                                             —*Jimmy Rogers*

93. BEST DAYS

1. Let me tell you baby
   You have seen your best days

   Let me tell you baby
   You have seen your best days

   I like you all right baby
   But I just can't stand your ways

2. I taken care of you baby
   You didn't even have a dime

Taken care of you baby
You didn't even have a dime

Yes you got your big money baby
It's when you won't pay me no mind

3. Come down here baby
Came here just to be with you

Came way down here baby
Honey just to be with you

Well darlin' we ain't got no money
Baby what you gonna do

4. Goodbye baby
Honey if you called it gone

Yeah goodbye baby
Baby if you called it gone

Yeah now you know I'm gon' worry baby
Yeah now you know it won't last long

—Baby Face Turner

94. HOLE IN THE WALL

1. My baby went out last night and got drunk
    Came home raisin' sand
    She had nerve enough to tell me "L.C.
    I found me a brand new man" she was at the Hole*
       in the Wall
    My baby ain't goin' to the Hole in the Wall no*
       more

---

line should continue but page prevents it from doing so.

Yes you know she's a sweet little girl
But I'm gonna have to let her go

2.   Yes you know my baby *does* a funny thing
          Starts jumping like a little cold chill
          But boy when she starts to blow she blows just
          Like a wagon wheel she was at the Hole in the Wall
My baby ain't goin' to the Hole in the Wall no more

Yes you know she's a sweet little girl
But I'm gonna have to let her go

3.   Yes you know I was walkin' down *Charlemagne*
          And I heard somebody squall
          You know I looked in man there was
          She was at the Hole in the Wall man
My baby ain't goin'
My baby ain't goin' to the Hole in the Wall no more

Yes you know she's a sweet little girl
But I'm gonna have to let her go

                                        —*L.C. Williams*

95. BAD LIFE BLUES

1. It's rainin' I know
   Baby and you treats me bad

   It's rainin' I know
   Baby and you treat me bad

   I got the worst old feelin'
   Woman I ever had

---

line should continue but page prevents it from doing so.

2. I've got rocks in my pillow
   My head won't rest no more

   Rocks in my pillow baby
   My head won't rest no more

   Spiders crawlin' up my wall
   Black snake crawlin' 'cross my floor

3. I got holes in my pocket
   Great big patches on my pants

   Holes in my pocket baby
   Great big patches on my pants

   I'm behind with my house rent
   I owe it all in 'vance

4. You know I feel like walkin'
   I feel like lyin' down

   I feel like walkin' baby
   I feel like lyin' down

   You know I feel like drinkin'
   But ain't no whiskey 'round

5. You hear that bell a-ringin'
   You hear that whistle blow

   You hear that bell a-ringin'
   You hear that whistle blow

   When I leave you baby
   I won't be back no more

6. Baby babe
   You brought it on yourself

   I'm leavin' you woman
   Don't want nobody else

—Smokey Hogg

96. I'M LEAVIN' YOU BABY

1. Well so long baby
   Well I've got to go

   Well so long baby
   Well I've got to go

   Where I'm stoppin' pretty mama baby
   You will never know

2. Well I'm leavin' you baby
   Please do the best you can

   Well I'm leavin' you mama
   Please do the best you can

   While I'm goin' to my woman you can
   Go back to your man

   (Well blow your harmonica son)

3. Well you'd better little woman
   You'd better change your mind

   Well you'd better little woman
   You'd better change your mind

   If you don't do no better I will
   Leave you sittin' here cryin'

—Lightnin' Slim

97. JUST CAN'T STAY

1. (Here I is again.
   Standin' on the corner of forty-seventh and South Parkway.
   I walked up to the little girl,

Said, "Can I have a word?" She said, "You can't do the*
   things that you used to do because I have a job makin'*
   much money as you do."
I say, "I'm so sorry, dear;
Your gettin' up at seven o'clock for one of them jobs will*
   wear your little fine self out."
She said, "May I have the last word?" I say, "Yes,*
   darlin'.")

Yes I'm goin'
Yes I'm goin'
And your cryin' won't
Make me stay
Yes the more you cry baby
Further you drive me away
Sure 'nough I just can't stay
Sure 'nough you drive me away
Sure 'nough you drive me away
Sure 'nough you drive me away

2. (You know, man,
   I was walkin' on the corner of thirty-first and *Charles*;
   I walked into a tavern and guess who I seen?
   Same little girl.
   I say, "Can I talk a little trash?"
   She said, "Talk a little trash? That means you have to*
      spend some cash."
   I say, "What you mean?" She say, "This is one thing and*
      that's for sure:
   Put somethin' on the bar excusin' your elbow."
   I said, "May I have the last word?" She say, "You may.")

Yes I'm goin'
To my baby's house
I'm gon' knock right up
On her door

---

*line should continue but page prevents it from doing so.

She said "I'm sorry now Willie boy
Don't live here no more
Sure 'nough you got to go
Sure 'nough you got to go
Sure 'nough you got go"

3. Yes if I
Was a catfish
Swimmin' in the hu-uh
Deep blue sea
I'd have all you pretty women
Fishin' after me
Sure 'nough after me
I mean after me
Sure 'nough after me

—Willie Nix

98. I'M GONNA QUIT YOU BABY

1.   *There's* _____ in my beans
            You burned up my bread
            The way you treat me woman I'll soon be dead*
                I'm gonna quit you pretty baby

I'm gonna quit you pretty baby
I'm gonna quit you pretty baby 'cause a woman*
    like you won't do

2.   You get up in the mornin'
            You slip on your robe
            The first thing you do is hit the road I'm gonna*
                quit you pretty baby

---

line should continue but page prevents it from doing so.

I'm gonna quit you pretty baby
I'm gonna quit you pretty baby 'cause a woman*
   like you won't do

3.   Take all my money buy whiskey and wine
          A-sittin' down drinkin' with a bunch of clowns*
             I'm gonna quit you pretty baby

I'm gonna quit you pretty baby
I'm gonna quit you pretty baby 'cause a woman*
   like you won't do

4.   I get back in the evenin' start to raisin' sand
          A-make me think you been out with another man*
             I'm gonna quit you pretty baby

I'm gonna quit you pretty baby
I'm gonna quit you pretty baby 'cause a woman*
   like you won't do

—*Silas Hogan*

99. SO LONG BLUES

1. So long
   Babe I think I stood enough

   So long
   Babe I think I stood enough

   You know the way you treat me baby
   I can't feel welcome here

2. You leave late in the evenin'
   You let the break of day bring you back

---

line should continue but page prevents it from doing so.

You leave late in the evenin'
You let the break of day bring you back

You must be think' I'm crazy baby
If I stay here and put up with that

3. So long
So long babe I say

So long
So long babe I'll say

You goin' to be sorry baby
You mistreated me this a-way

—Silas Hogan

100. ONE OF THESE DAYS

1. One of these days
You're gon' need my help again

One of these days
You'r gon' need my help again

You know good as I been to you darlin'
You gon' think about me ever' now and then

2.   You know I brought my paycheck home on Friday
Like a good man should
Wasn't able to buy you no diamond
I did the best that I could but one of these days
You're gon' need my help again

Good as I been to you darlin'
You're gon' think about me ever' now and then

3.   I took you downtown
         Tried to buy you ever 'thing you need
         You throwed away all of my money
         You called that chicken feed
   But one of these days
   You're gon' need my help again

   You know good as I been to you darlin'
   You're gon' think about me ever' now and then

4.   You know I liable to wake up one of these*
             mornings
         I liable to lose my head
         I'll snap that old 32-20 in your face
         And the barrel'll turn cherry red
   One of these days
   You're gon' need my help again

   You know good as I been to you darlin'
   You gon' think about me ever' now and then

                                        —*Big Boy Spires*

101. WEDNESDAY EVENIN' BLUES

1. You know she left me one Wednesday
   When the sun was sinkin' low

   Oooh she left me that Wednesday evenin'
   When the sun was sinkin' low

   My baby don't know how she hurt me
   She made me feel so bad

---

line should continue but page prevents it from doing so.

2.   My baby told me
            "I told you Johnny
            A long time ago
            You don't stop your old ways
            Gonna leave you baby
            You thought one thing
            I love you too hard
            To leave you
            But now
            The day have come
            You love me
            I don't love you
            You did me so bad
            You drove my love away
            But not I'm leavin'
            Mm
            Leavin'
            The day is Wednesday
            I'm leavin' on this day"
            Yeah ev'ryday people
            Ev'ryday on Wednesday
            I think about my baby
       You know she left me
       When the sun was sinkin' low

Mm mm mmm Mmmmm mm m oh oh oh oh oh

3.   She slipped down and told me
            She said "Johnny
            You can do a girl so bad
            She can love you
            A length of time
            If you don't change your mind
            The girl get tired
            Her love go away
            But now I'm tired
            And you in love"
       I said "Baby please don't go
       I have changed my mind"

That was one Wednesday evenin'
When the sun was
               sinkin' low

Mm mm mm Mm mm mm mm m mmm mmm m
Mmm mmm m mmm mmm mmm mm mmm*
  mmm mmm

—*John Lee Hooker*

102. NO NIGHTS BY MYSELF

1. Mmm
      I'm not goin' to
  Spend another night by myself

  Lord I'm not going to
  Spend 'nother
            night by myself
  If I don't
      find my baby
  I'll have to carry
          somebody else

2. I set up all night last night
  Haven't slept a wink today

  All night last night
  I haven't slept a wink today

  I couldn't find my baby
  She's gone
        too far away

---

line should continue but page prevents it from doing so.

3. Mmm Mm Mmmm Mm
Mmm Mmm mmm mmm
Whoa whoa whoa
She must have
                left town
She left town
(She had to've left town)

—*Sonny Boy Williamson*

103. YOU CAN'T TELL THEM WHERE I'M GOING

1. You know the sun is rising
People my trunk is packed

   Yes the sun is rising
People and my trunk is packed

   When I leave this town
Man I won't be back

2. You please tell my friends
You can't tell 'em where I'm goin'

   You can tell my friends
But you can't tell 'em where I'm goin'

   Just tell 'em I left a no-good woman
That drove me from home

3. You know my life is good baby
I try to do ev'rything that's right

   Yeah my life is good
I try to do ev'rything that's right

   If you don't be lucky today
Don't blame me tonight

—*Smokey Hogg*

104. I TRIED

1. Now listen all you friends
   That ever heard a record I made
   Remember just one thing Lord I did ev'rything that I could

2. Don't thank me friends
   Just thank only one man Mister Brunie Besman

3. That was the first man
   That give me my chance
   Name of the place was
   Pan-American Record Company Lord I tried
   I tried to do the best I can

4. I'm sorry I couldn't play
   The piece you liked best
   I had to play at the blues Lord that's the first thing I know
   But I tried
   I tried to do the best I can

5. If you peoples understand
   Ev'ry man have to crawl
   Ev'ry baby have to crawl Lord
   Before he walk
   I've tried
   Lord I tried to do the best I can
   (For Mister Brunie now)

6. Say hey
   Let me tell you somethin' friend
   Lord you don't know how good *he tells me* poor Mac*
       when you
   Lord when you tryin'
   When you're tryin' to do the

---

*line should continue but page prevents it from doing so.

7. Says now you watch out
   The window when the man says
   Now it's time for you to cut your
   Voice off then Mister Sylvester you tried
   Lord you tried to do the

8. I want you to excuse
   All the mistakes in this song
   Lord 'cause this is the last one I'll ever play maybe but I'll*
       try
   Lord I'll try to do the best I can

9. So long
   I got to go
   Lord 'cause somebody waitin' on me in the room behind me
   But I tried
   Lord I tried to do the best I can

—*Sylvester Cotton*

105. GOT TO LET YOU GO

1. (Let's go.
   Hey, Caldonia!
   Now where in the world has you been?
   Confound your soul.
   I been here all the afternoon tryin' to get somethin' to eat,*
       you downtown there
   Drinkin' wine and feelin' fine.
   When I come home from work it's all I heard,
   This cat's told me that he stole my wife downtown there,
   Hangin' around them beer gardens drinkin' wine and*
       feelin' mighty fine.

---

*line should continue but page prevents it from doing so.

Ain't no use you standing up there looking like three*
     shades in the wind,
'Cause I think one of these is gonna kill and knock you*
     on your knees.
Baby we all got to go to jail, course I don't care 'cause I'm*
     tired of messin' with you.
You know when I first married you babe I told you I*
     would do everything I could for you.
Now you're buying clothes, a big automobile, now look*
     what you're doin',
Ridin' around here with these cats in these long-draped*
     pants and these long-toed shoes,
Tryin' to tell me about
You gon' have plenty of money!
Now you know that ain't gon' never work with the be-bop*
     boy.)
'Cause I'm gon' let you go
Yes I'm gon' let you go
(You ain't no good no more.)
I'm gonna let you go
I can't stand your ways

2. (Now look at you there, baby,
     Talkin' bout you got plenty of money and your toes all*
          stickin' out there,
     Your hair all nappy there and your clothes all torn!
     Where in the world you been?
     I'm workin' hard every day and you eatin' up all my meat*
          and won't get up and cook me nothin' to eat,
     I'm diggin' and slavin' and cuttin' up that concrete,
     I'm just about got cold feet, I'm 'bout to let that woman go.
     Hang around these beer gardens and these garbage cans.
     Now look, I'm gonna talk about you now.)
     Yes I told your mother

---

*line should continue but page prevents it from doing so.

Yes I told your brother
Yes I told your brother
Got to let you go

3. (Now look here her hair's all nappy there and her toes all*
    stickin' out there,
   She ain't had her hair fixed nearly in about seven years,*
    boys.
   Hangin' around these garbage cans and everything.
   I might get cold feet, I'll probably let that woman go.)
   Yes I don't love you no more
   I don't love you no more
   I don't love you no more
   I got to let you go

—*Joe Hill Louis*

106. I BETTER GO NOW

1. (Yes baby)
   I better go now
   I better go now baby

   I better go now
   Before I get out my blade

   You done spent my money
   Throwed it all away

2. I had that money
   To buy us a home

   Yes I had that money
   To buy us a home

---

line should continue but page prevents it from doing so.

When I come home
The money was gone

I better go now
Before I get out my blade

3. There's many people
Dead and in the grave

Yes there's a-many people
Dead and in the grave

I better leave you now darling
Before I get out my blade

4. I had that money
To buy you a diamond ring

I had that money
To buy you a diamond ring

I found out
You give it to your other man

I better go now
I better go now

—*Howlin' Wolf*

107. CRYING WON'T HELP YOU

1.   No matter what you say baby
        No matter what you do
        The way you treated me baby
        Is comin' back home to you
   And cryin' won't help you
   Cryin' won't help you
   Cryin' won't help you baby
   'Cause you've been so mean to me

2.   You must remember baby
           No matter where you go
           Watch those seeds you scatter baby
           Because you're gonna reap just what you sow and
Cryin' won't help you
Your cryin' won't help you
Cryin' won't help you baby
'Cause you have been so mean to me

3.   This way you're treatin' me baby
           I cannot understand
           So I'm gon' leave you baby and let you
           Do the best you can and
Cryin' won't help you
Cryin' won't help you
Cryin' won't help you baby
'Cause you have been so mean to me
(Dig these jives now man.)

4.   Before I leave you darlin'
           I just want to shake your hand
           I'm goin' back to my woman
           And let you go back to your man but remember
Cryin' won't help you
Cryin' won't help you
Cryin' won't help you baby
'Cause you have been so mean to me

—Tampa Red

108. EARLY MORNING

1. Early in the morning
   Catch the morning train

   Early in the morning
   Catch the morning train

Says my baby
                done quit me and my life don't
                                    seem the*

    same

2. Going in the morning
   Sure do hate to go

   Going in the morning
   Sure do hate to go

   Says I may stop in Texas and I may stop down by
                                        Mexico

3. Whoa I'm cryin'
   Don't have to cry no more

   I been cryin'
   Folks don't have to cry no more

   Says my baby
                has done told me that she don't want
                                        me no*

      more

4. Shetland in Texas
   He's already trained

   Shetland down in Texas
   He's already trained

   And if he don't
                travel to suit you
                            tighten up
                                    on the rein

                                    —*Floyd Jones*

---

line should continue but page prevents it from doing so.

109. TRAIN TIME

1. It was early one morning
   Just about four o'clock

   Man it was early one morning
   Just about four o'clock

   You know something crawl into my bedroom
   And begin to reel and rock

2. Throw your lovin' arms around me
   Like a circle around the sun

   Throw your lovin' arms around me baby
   Like a circle around the sun

   Now tell your daddy
   How you want your rollin' done

3. Lord I woke up this morning
   All I had was gone

   Man I woke up this morning
   All I had was gone

   I didn't have nobody
   To talk baby talk to me

4. Well now it's train time here
   I believe I've got to go

   Well now it's train time here people
   Lord I believe I've got to go

   Well I've got to go and leave you
   All I had is gone

—*Sunnyland Slim*

110. TAKE IT EASY BABY

1.   Now look here baby you better start right
               You went out last night and stayed all night
     You better take it easy baby
     Better take it easy baby
     You better take it easy baby 'cause I don't like the way*
          you do

2.   Now I give you my money you left me cold in*
               hand
               Taken my money start to raisin' cane
     You better take it easy baby
     Better take it easy baby
     You better take it easy baby 'cause I don't like the way*
          you do

3.   Now I give you my money and I bought you*
               clothes
               Now you want to put me out doors
     You better take it easy baby
     Better take it easy baby
     You better take it easy baby 'cause I don't like the way*
          you do

4.   Now I give you my money when the time was hard
               You want to quit me baby soon as I lose my job
     Better take it easy baby
     Better take it easy baby
     You better take it easy baby 'cause I don't like the way*
          you do
     (All right.)

---

*line should continue but page prevents it from doing so.

5.   Now I'm goin' away to leave won't be back till fall
         Times don't get no better ain't coming' back at all
   You better take it easy baby
   Better take it easy baby
   Better take it easy baby 'cause I don't like the way you do

6.   Well I'm goin' away to leave won't be back no*
            more
         Better stop hangin' around my door
   You better take it easy baby
   Better take it easy baby
   Better take it easy babe
   Better take it easy baby 'cause I don't like the way you do

— *Robert Nighthawk*

111.   GOIN' DOWN HIGHWAY 51

1. I'm gon' get up in the morning
   Goin' down highway 51

   Get up in the mornin'
   Goin' down highway 51

   Miss Fannie Mae's my sweet woman
   And she don't pay me no mind

2. Yes she's up this morning
                          lord lord lord
   And she rode the B. & O.

   Mm mm mm
   Mm mm mm mm mm mmmmm
   Mm mm mm

---

line should continue but page prevents it from doing so.

Yes she left me
And she rode that
          B. & O.

3. When she was leavin, lord lord lord
   She would even lord shake my hand

   Someday I will meet you
   When your troubles get like mine

   Mm mm mmm mm mm

                              — *John Lee Hooker*

112. BYE BYE BIRD

1. Bye bye bird
   Bye bye bird
   Bye bye bird
   Bye bye bird
   Bye bye
            bird
              I'm gone

2. Bird I'm goin'
   Bird I'm goin'
   Bird I'm goin'
   Bird I'm goin'
   I'm goin' to try to find
                   a happy home

                      — *Sonny Boy Williamson*

VII

Sometime I Was Goin' So Fast
That I Just Couldn't See The Road

"Lord I went down 18 highway,
I went down in my Dynaflow.

Lord sometime I was goin' so fast
That I just couldn't see the road."

—*Little Willie Foster, "Falling Rain Blues" (transcription 119).*

113. HARD TIMES

1. Times done got hard
   Well I b'lieve I'll go back home

   Yes the times done got hard
   I believe I'll go back home

   Well I'm goin' back
   Where I can raise

   hogs and corn

2. On that next train South
   You can look for me home

   On that next train South
   You can look for me home

   Well I want to give a big

   celebration
   Well in the place

   where I was born

3. Well goodbye goodbye
   Tell e-

   v'rybody I'm gone

   Yes goodbye yes goodbye
   Tell ev'rybody I'm gone

   Well if times don't get better
   You will find little Johnny at home

— Johnny Fuller

114. I CAN'T BE SATISFIED

1.   Well I'm goin' away to leave
      Won't be back no more
      Goin' back down South child don't you want to go

Woman I'm troubled
I be all worried mind

Well babe I just can't be satisfied
And I just can't keep from crying'

2.   Well I feel like snappin'
            Pistol in your face
            I'm gon' let some graveyard lord be her restin' place
    Lord I'm troubled
    I be all worried mind

    Well babe I can't never be satisfied
    And I just can't keep from cryin'
    (Play)

3.   Well now all in my sleep
            Hear my doorbell ring
            Lookin' for my baby I can see not a doggone thing
    Lord I was troubled
    I was all worried mind

    Well honey I couldn't never be satisfied
    And I just couldn't keep from cryin'

4.   Well I know my little old babe
            She gon' jump and shout
            That old train be late man Lord and I come*
                runnin' out
    I'll be troubled
    I be all worried mind

    Well honey ain't no way in the world for me to be satisfied
    And I just can't keep from cryin'

                                        — *Muddy Waters*

---

*line should continue but page prevents it from doing so.

115. DOWN HOME GIRL

1. Well I'm a down home girl
   And I'm tired of fooling with you

   Well I'm a down home girl
   And I'm tired of fooling with you

   That's why I'm gonna leave you baby
   'Cause I've got those down home blues

2. When I go to Memphis
   I'm gonna walk down on Beale and Third

   Well when I go to Memphis
   I'm gonna walk down on Beale and Third

   So me and my old-time friends
   Can set down and swap a few words

3. Well when I leave Chicago
   I'm gonna buy my ticket straight on through

   Well when I leave Chicago
   I'm gonna buy my ticket straight on through

   And say "Hurry engineer
   'Cause I've got those down home blues"

4. Well I go back home
   I believe my luck will change

   Well if I go back home
   I believe my luck will change

   Then I will find me a man
   Wheee—hoo that really knows the game

— *Memphis Minnie*

116. THE END

1. Well I woke up soon one morning
   I had the blues all 'round my bed

   Yes I woke up soon one morning
   I had the blues all 'round my bed

   Well I reached
                  for my baby
   And I got these
                  blues instead

2. I walked the street late at night
   Till my feet turned
                  soakin' wet

   Yes I walked the street late at night
   Till my feet turned
                  soakin' wet

   Well I asked
                  all my friends
   Haven't heard talk of my
                  baby yet

3. Just wrote a letter back home to the boys
   Askin' them to please pray
                  for my sins

   Yes I wrote a letter home
                  to the boys
   Askin' them to please pray
                  for my sins

   Well I'm headed down toward the ocean
   I believe that this
                  is the end

                              — *James Reed*

117. ON THE ROAD AGAIN

1.   Whoa
                    kinda worried and cryin'
          Boys I'm out on
                              the road again on the road again
    Worried about my baby o^{oo}oo
    Worried about my babyooo^{ooo}oo oo
    Don't feel like I
                    have a fr^{iend}

2.   Whoa Lord
                    I had to travel
          Boys
                  in the rain and snow in the rain and snow
    My baby had quit me^{ee}ooo
    My baby had quit me^{ee}ooo
    Have no place to go^{o}

3.   Whoa
                    take the hint from me boys
          Please don't
                      cry no more don't cry no more
    Gonna be early in the morn^{ooo}oo
    Walkin' in the old rain and sno^{ow}

4.   Whoa
                    Sunnyland did you hear
          A church bell
                          ring and tone did you hear the*
              church bells ring and tone

---

line should continue but page prevents it from doing so.

My little
baby^{ooo}oo
My little baby^{ooo}oo
Boys
     she's dead and gone

—Floyd Jones

118. GRIEVANCE BLUES

1. Grievin' over you babe
   Darlin' I have almost lost my mind

   I been grievin' over you baby
   Till I have almost lost my mind

   Yes you know it have settled on my brain
   And it almost drove me blind

2. You know I can't eat for thinkin'
   You know and I can't hardly see for cryin'

   You know I can't eat for thinkin'
   I can't hardly see for cryin'

   Yes you know it have settled on my brain
   And it almost have drove me blind

3. I done grieved over you woman
   Till I done got weak in my knees

   I done grieved over you baby till I done
   Got weak in my knees

   Yes I'm just wand'rin around in this world and I ain't got
   Nobody to care for me

—Lightnin' Hopkins

119. FALLING RAIN BLUES

1. Got up this mornin'
   Lookin' through my windowpane

   Got up this mornin'
   Lookin' through my windowpane

   Lord I could see my baby
   Walkin' out in the showers of rain

2. Lord my baby's gone
   She's gone down in the old shady grove

   Lord my baby's gone
   She's gone down in the old shady grove

   Now that's where they carried my baby
   Carried her down to the burying ground
   (All right Floyd)

3. Lord I went down 18 highway
   I went down in my Dynaflow

   Lord I went down 18 highway
   I went down in my Dynaflow

   Lord sometime I was goin' so fast
   That I just couldn't see the road

—*Little Willie Foster*

120 GOIN' BACK AND TALK TO MAMA

1. Yes man I was born March the fifteenth
   You know the year of nineteen hundred and twelve

   Yes I was born March the fifteenth
   Boys nineteen hundred and twelve

Yes you know ever since that day
Poor Lightnin' ain't been doin' so well

2.   Yes I'm goin' back and talk to Mama
              Just to see what Mama say
              So she will make me think about my old home seat
              And the places that I used to play you know I'm
Goin' back and talk to Mama
Just to see what will poor Mama say

Yeah so she can make me remember
Old places where I used to play

3.   When I go to talk to my Mama
              These is the words that I'm gon' say
              "Just show me the old places I used to be Mama*
                 and the places I used to play" you know I'm
Talk to my Mama gon' ask her
Whoa 'bout the places I used to play

Yes I'm often thinkin' about
Where I used to lay

—Lightnin' Hopkins

121. SHELBY COUNTY BLUES

1. My home in Shelby county
   That's where I long to be

   My home in Shelby county
   That's where I long to be

   I got womens down there
   Mean the world and all to me

---

line should continue but page prevents it from doing so.

2. You take my Shelby county women
   And stand them all in a line

   You take my Shelby county women
   And stand them all in a line

   You can count them out
   One two three four five six seven eight nine
   (Play me some blues boy you know how I feel
   I'm goin' back to old Shelby county if I don't stay but one*
      day)

3. I've got a gal on my gal
   I got a kid gal on my doggone kid

   I got a gal on my gal
   I got a kid gal on my doggone kid

   Sometime that gal gets so boogie-assed
   She can hardly keep it hid

—*Little Johnny Jones*

122. SEVENTY-FOUR BLUES

1. Yes I'm goin' home in the mornin'
   I'm goin' to ride number seventy-four

   Yes I'm goin' home in the mornin'
   I'm goin' to ride number seventy-four

   Yes if I ever get back up North peoples
   I ain't comin' down South no more

2. Seventy-four is just a freight train
   But it got ways just like a man

---

*line should continue but page prevents it from doing so.

Well seventy-four girl is just a freight train but it
It got ways just like a man

Well it'll take your sweet little woman
Boys and put you down cold in hand

3. Well I rode number seventy-four
Boys and the rain was fallin' down

Yes I rode number seventy-four
Boys and the rain was fallin' down

Well you know I got awful cold and chilly
Boys but I was Chicago bound

4. Yes if you live in the country write to me
If you're downtown you can telephone

Yes if you live in the country write to me darlin'
If you're downtown girl you can telephone

Well you know I just want to keep in touch with you*
   baby whilst I'm
Tryin' to *beat* my way back home

                                  —*Willie Love*

123. THE GOAT

1.
           There was a animal
           Called a goat
           He butted his way
           Out of the Supreme Court
    Said "Let him go"
    Yeah said "Let him go

---

line should continue but page prevents it from doing so.

Because he butt so hard
Till you can't use him in our court no more"

2.   Judge give him five hours to
          Get out of town
          He got five miles down the road
          And committed another crime
          That's when the high sheriff
          Happened to be comin' along
          And caught the billy goat eatin' up an
          Old farmer's corn
          High sheriff taken the billy goat to the
          County jail
          But the desk sergeant said that
          "I'll go his bail
          Let him go"

3.   A medicine doctor bought the billy goat
          Had a great big stage show
          The billy goat got mad and butt him right down
          In the *lonesome* floor
So let him go
Please please let him go

Because he butt so hard
Till I can't use him in our
                    Court no more
Ohh

—*Sonny Boy Williamson*

124. LOUISIANA BLUES

1. I'm goin' down in Louisiana
   Baby behind the sun

   I'm goin' down in Louisiana
   Honey behind the sun

Well you know I just found out
My trouble just begun

2. I'm goin' down in New Orleans, hmm
Get me a mojo hand

I'm goin' down in New Orleans
Get me a mojo hand
                (Take me with you when you go.)

I'm gon' show all you good-looking women
Just how to treat your man
                (Let's go back to New Orleans, boys.)

—Muddy Waters

125. GOOD EVENING EVERYBODY

1. Good evening everybody
Tell me how do you do

Good evening everybody
Tell me how do you do

I'm one of the
                artists of Chess
Come out to work a little

2. Goodbye
        hello
                goodbye
Goodbye
        hello
                goodbye
I didn't come
                here to stay I just
Come here
            to work awhile

3. This morning
   I just dropped in your town

   This morning
   I just dropped in your town

   I'm in the studio over in Chicago
   Tryin' to knock these blues around

—*Sonny Boy Williamson*

Note to the Lyrics

In these notes, the song title appears first, followed by the singer's name, the place and date of the recording, the record company, and the issue number of the original release. If there is an album reissue, the record company name appears next, followed by the issue number, and the title of the album containing the song. Finally, I have listed the name of the copyright holder, if known, and explanatory information about the text.

I have omitted biographical information about the singers. Further biographical information can be found in *Blues Who's Who*, the periodicals *Living Blues* and *Blues Unlimited*, on album record jackets, and in the books in Suggestions for Further Reading.

I have refrained from cross-referencing versions and variants of lyrics printed in this anthology as they appear on record or in other printed collections. To paraphrase the ballad scholar Bertrand Bronson, diligence here makes an amusing game for the specialist, but produces a tangled thicket whose purpose all too frequently becomes obscure for the general reader. Bronson was writing about ballads; in blues, where no narrative thread binds stanzas in consecutive order, and where traditional phrases, lines, and verses float easily from one singer and song to the next, the tangle becomes so thick that it is usually impossible to determine from the lyrics alone the paths of transmission. Meaningful cross-referencing, which must include tens of thousands of recorded performances of blues lyrics, is ultimately a task for the computer.

I Down Home

1. "Down in Mississippi" by Jimmy Reed. Chicago, 1962, Vee Jay 616, Archive of Folk and Jazz 234, *Jimmy Reed*. ©1962 Conrad Music, a division of Arc Music Corp., 110 East 59th Street, New York, NY 10022; used by permission. Release of this record was delayed for two years after

it was recorded. *Boll weevil wearin' overalls*: personification of the cotton pest associates him with the farmers and indicates he is a match for the tall cotton. *Late over in the evenin'*: around 5 p.m.

2. "Have You Ever" by "Mercy Dee" (Mercy D. Walton). Los Angeles, 1955, Flair 1078, Kent 9012, *West Coast Blues*. ©1972 Modern Music Publ. Co. 5810 S. Normandie Ave., Los Angeles, CA 90044; used by permission. The word omitted in verse 2 may be the name of an accompanying musician.

3. "Big Boss Man" by Jimmy Reed. Chicago, 1960, Vee Jay 380, Kent 537, *Root of the Blues*. ©1960 Conrad Music, a division of Arc Music Corp., BMI; used by permission. This best-seller crossed over from the rhythm 'n' blues playlists to become very popular on the white rock 'n' roll radio stations.

4. "Grosebeck Blues" (take 3) by "Lightnin' " (Sam) Hopkins. Houston, CA. 1947, Unissued*, Arhoolie 2010, *Lightnin' Hopkins, Early Recordings, Vol. 2*. According to Chris Strachwitz, owner-producer of Arhoolie and Blues Classics Records, the first take was brief and incomplete; the second and third were issued on Arhoolie 2010; the fourth was issued on Verve (LP) 8543. Hopkins recorded it again in different form in 1959 for Folkways, which gave it the Verve title, "Penitentiary Blues". The word omitted in verse 1 may be the name of a Texas penitentiary.

5. "Tim Moore's Farm" by "Lightnin' " (Sam) Hopkins. Houston, 1947, Gold Star 640, Arhoolie 2010, Lightnin' Hopkins, Early Recordings, Vol. 2. This song, more commonly known as "Tom Moore's Farm," circulates in several variants, principally among Texas singers. For other recordings of this interesting lyric, compare Johnny Shines's "Mr. Tom Green's Farm" on Testament (LP) 2212 with a long version recorded by Texas songster Mance Lipscomb, on Blues Classics BC–16. This indictment of the paternalistic plantation sharecropping system is one of the few recorded blues songs to protest directly against racial discrimination and resulting social conditions. *I'll save you from the pen*: plantation owners could influence local sheriffs and justices of the peace.

6. "Trouble At Home Blues" by Silas Hogan. Crowley, Louisiana, ca. 1962, Excello 2221, Blue Horizon 2431 008, *Trouble at Home*. ©1962 Excellorec Music Co., 1011 Woodland St., Nashville, TN 37206; used by permission.

7. "Burnin' Hell" by John Lee Hooker. Detroit, 1949, Sensation 21. ©1970 Venice Music and LaCienega Music Company, c/o ATV Music Corp., BMI; used by permission; all rights reserved. The second and third

---

*Recorded, but never released on a 78 or 45 rpm record.

verses seem to have been improvised spontaneously as in black old-time prayer and preaching. Although Hooker uses this free form technique on occasion, it is uncommon generally in recorded postwar blues.

8. "Bad Boy" by John Lee Hooker. Detroit, 1953, Modern 942, Crown 295, *Folk Blues. Mmm, etc.* Hooker hums the melody he plays.

9. "Cotton Crop Blues" by James Cotton. Memphis, 1954, Sun 206, London 8265, *The Blues Came Down from Memphis.*

10. "Dark Muddy Bottom" by "Mercy Dee" (Mercy D. Walton). Los Angeles, 1954, Specialty 481, Specialty 2149, *Dark Muddy Bottom Blues.*

11. "Down Child" by John Lee Hooker. Detroit 1953, Modern 923, Crown 295, *Folk Blues.* See note on "Burnin' Hell," No. 7.

II I'm the Sweetest Man in Town

12. "She Fooled Me" by Harvey Hill, Jr. Detroit, ca. 1952, Blues Classics 23, *Juke Joint Blues. Jivin':* pretending, lying. *Kid:* young lover. *You may not keep it hid.* you may not keep the love affair secret.

13. "Evil Blues": by "Lil' Son" (Melvin) Jackson. Houston, 1949, Gold Star 663, Highway 51 103, *Texas-Louisiana. Sanctified*: member of the Church of God in Christ. The lyrics are ironic.

14. "Mattie Mae" by "Baby Boy" (Robert) Warren. Detroit, ca. 1953, Blue Lake 106, Blues Classics 12, *Detroit Blues.* Derived from John Lee "Sonny Boy" Williamson's "Mattie Mae Blues" and identical with another version, "Hello Stranger," which Warren recorded on JVB 26 at approximately the same time. *Calvin*: Calvin Frazier, accompanying guitarist.

15. "Going Fishing" by Jimmy Reed. Chicago, 1964, Vee Jay 1095, *Jimmy Reed at Soul City.* ©1964, Conrad Music, a division of Arc Music, BMI; used by permission.

16. "Kissing in the Dark" by "Memphis Minnie" (Minnie McCoy Lawlar). Chicago(?), 1954, JOB 1101, Boogie Disease 101–102, *Take a Little Walk with Me. Business*: personal affairs.

17. "Please Don't Think I'm Nosey" by "Baby Boy" (Robert) Warren. Detroit, 1949, Staff 709, pwb 5, *Detroit.*

18. "Baker Shop Boogie" by Willie Nix. Memphis, 1953, Sun 179, London 8265, *The Blues Came Down from Memphis. Jelly roll*; flesh around abdomen, thighs, buttocks; hence, sexual equipment. *Boogie*: dance; additionally, the motions of sexual intercourse.

19. "Money, Marbles and Chalk" by "Jimmy Rogers" (James A. Lane). Chicago, 1951, Chess 1476, Chess 407, *Chicago Bound.* © 1965 Arc Music Corp., BMI; used by permission.

20. "Rough Dried Woman" by "Big Mac." 1966, Ronn 8, Pye International 28142, *Blues from Bayou.*

21. "Alley Special" by Wright Holmes. Houston, 1947, Miltone 5221, Blues Classics 7, *Country Blues Classics, Vol. 3*. Like the baking metaphor in "Baker Shop Boogie," the comparisons with farm animals refer to sex acts.

22. "Lonesome Cabin" by "Sonny Boy Williamson" (Rice Miller). Chicago, 1960, Checker 956, Chess 1536, *Bummer Road.* ©1960 Arc Music Corp., BMI; used by permission.

23. "Eyesight to the Blind" by "Sonny Boy Williamson" (Rice Miller). Jackson, Mississippi, 1951, Trumpet 129, Blues Classics 9, *The Original Sonny Boy Williamson.* ©1951 (renewed) Arc Music Corp., BMI; used by permission. *Lay it on me, we got to get out of here now, etc.*: encouraging patter spoken to accompanists.

24. "Good News" by "Muddy Waters" (McKinley Morganfield). Chicago, 1957, Chess 1667, Syndicate Chapter 002, *Good News.* ©1957 Arc Music Corp., BMI; used by permission. *Whoa do it again*: cue to accompanists.

25. "Mr. Highway Man" by "Howlin' Wolf" (Chester Burnett). Chicago, 1953, Chess 1510, Syndicate Chapter 003, *Goin' Back Home.* ©1972 Arc Music Corp., BMI; used by permission. *Check my oil, long ragged machine, etc.*: in the blues lyric tradition, riding and related activities constitute an extended sexual metaphor.

26. "Santa Claus" by "Sonny Boy Williamson" (Rice Miller). Chicago, 1960, Unissued, Chess 1536, *Bummer Road.* ©1970 Arc Music Corp., BMI; used by permission.

27. "Good Thing Blues" by "Doctor Ross" (Isaiah Ross). Memphis, 1954, Unissued, Arhoolie 1065, *Doctor Ross: Early Recordings.*

28. "New Crawlin' King Snake" by "Howlin' Wolf" (Chester Burnett). Chicago, 1966, Chess 1968, Chess 418, *Change My Way. Crawlin' king snake*: in the blues lyric tradition, a snake is a figure for the penis.

29. "Man Around My Door" by Grace Brim. Chicago, 1952, J.O.B. 117, Juke Joint 1501, *Blues Is Killing Me.*

30. "Katie Mae" by "Lightnin' " (Sam) Hopkins. Los Angeles, 1946, Alladin 167, Imperial 12259, *Best of the Blues, Vol. 2.*

31. "Tell Me Baby" by Silas Hogan. Crowley, Louisiana, ca. 1965, Unissued, Flyright 518, *Rooster Crowed for Day.*

32. "Honey Bee" by "Muddy Waters" (McKinley Morganfield). Chicago, 1951, Chess 1468, Chess 1427, *The Best of Muddy Waters.* ©1959 Arc Music Corp., BMI; used by permission.

33. "Henry's Swing Club" by John Lee Hooker. Detroit, ca. 1949, Unissued, Specialty 2127, *Goin' Down Highway 51.* ©Venice Music and LaCienega Music Co., c/o ATV Music Corp., BMI; used by permission; all rights reserved.

34. "Miss Loretta" by "Lightnin' " (Sam) Hopkins. Houston, ca.

1948, Unissued, Imperial 12211, *Lightnin' Hopkins and the Blues. Sugar mama*: sweet sex partner.

35. "Long Way From Texas" by "Lightnin' " (Sam) Hopkins. New York, 1950, SIW 611, Mainstream 311, *The Blues. Seed*: seen. *Waitin' on*: waiting for.

36. "Sweetest Woman" by Joe Hill Louis. West Memphis, 1954, Unissued, White Label 9955, *Going Down to Louisiana. Rampart Street*: street in New Orleans famous for its nightlife.

37. "So Sad to be Lonesome" by "Sonny Boy Williamson" (Rice Miller). Chicago(?), 1962, Unissued, Rarity 1, *Last Sessions*.

III I Can't Do It All By Myself

38. "It's Your Life" by Johnny Fuller. Oakland, 1954, Unissued, Kent 9003, *California Blues.* ©1970 Modern Music Publ. Co., BMI; used by permission.

39. "Take It Easy Baby" by Nat Terry. Dallas(?), 1951, Imperial 5150, pwb 4, *Texas*.

40. "Help Me" by "Sonny Boy Williamson" (Rice Miller). Chicago, 1963, Checker 1036, Chess 1509, *More Real Folk Blues.* ©1963 Arc Music Corp., BMI; used by permission.

41. "This Old Life" by "Sonny Boy Williamson" (Rice Miller). Chicago, 1960, Unissued, Chess 1536, *Bummer Road*.

42. "Your Funeral And My Trial" by "Sonny Boy Williamson" (Rice Miller). Chicago, 1958, Checker 894. ©1958 Arc Music Corp., BMI; used by permission.

43. "Build A Cave" by "Mr. Honey" (David "Honeyboy" Edwards). Houston, 1951, Artist Record Company 102, Blues Classics 23, *Juke Joint Blues*. Probably derived from Arthur Crudup's earlier song, "I'm Gonna Dig Myself a Hole," but a superior lyric. *Class card*: draft classification card. *Reds*: Communists.

44. "War News Blues" by "Lightnin' " (Sam) Hopkins. Houston, 1951, Unissued, Kent 9008, *A Legend in His Own Time.* ©1071 Modern Music Publ. Co., BMI; used by permission.

45. "Don't Lose Your Eye" by "Sonny Boy Williamson" (Rice Miller). Chicago, 1955, Unissued, Chess 417, *One Way Out.* ©1976 Arc Music Corp., BMI; used by permission.

46. "School Days" by Floyd Jones. Chicago, 1948, Tempotone,(?) Nighthawk 102, *Chicago Slickers*.

47. "Still a Fool" by "Muddy Waters" (McKinley Morganfield). Chicago, 1951, Chess 1480, Chess 1427, *The Best of Muddy Waters.* ©1959 Arc Music Corp., BMI; used by permission.

48. "My Fault" by "Muddy Waters" (McKinley Morganfield). Chi-

cago, 1951, Chess 1480, Syndicate Chapter 001, *Back in the Early Days, Vol. 1.* ©1974 Arc Music Corp., BMI; used by permission.

49. "Coffee Blues" by "Lightnin' " (Sam) Hopkins. New York, 1950, Jax 635, Mainstream 311, *The Blues.* Unusual because he sings it from a child's perspective.

IV The Living Have Gone So High

50. "Democrat Blues" by "Bo Bo" (J. P.) Jenkins. Detroit, 1954, Chess 1565, Blues Classics 6, *Country Blues Classics, Vol. 2.*

51. "Stockyard Blues" by Floyd Jones. Chicago, 1947, Old Swingmaster 22, Blues Classics 8, *Chicago Blues. Feet*: pigs' feet. *Snook*: Snooky Pryor, accompanist on harmonica. *Moody*: Moody Jones, accompanist on bass.

52. "Things Are So Slow" by J. B. Hutto. Chicago, 1954, Chance 1165, Blues Classics 8, *Chicago Blues. Finance*: bank or loan company.

53. "Tough Times" by John Brim. Chicago, 1953, Parrott 799, Blues Classics 8, *Chicago Blues.* ©1970 Arc Music Corp., BMI; used by permission. *Eddie*: Eddie Taylor, accompanist on guitar.

54. "Repossession Blues" by "Lightnin' Leon". Memphis, 1960, Rita 1005, Blues Classics 23, *Juke Joint Blues. Bel-Air*: Chevrolet automobile.

55. "Everybody Wants To Know" by J. B. Lenoir. Chicago, 1956, Unissued, Chess 410, *Natural Man.* © 1970 Arc Music Corp., BMI; Used by permission.

56. "Candy Kitchen" by "Lightnin' " (Sam) Hopkins. Houston, 1951, RPM 378, Kent 9008, *A Legend in His Own Time.* © 1971 Modern Music Publ. Co., BMI, used by permission. *W.P. and A.: Works Progress Administration:* a New Deal agency. Hopkins recorded a slightly different version, "I Just Don't Care," released on Imperial (LP) 9211.

57. "Living in the Whitehouse" by Johnny Shines. Chicago, 1953, Unissued, Boogie Disease 101–102, *Take a Little Walk with Me. Ike*: President Dwight D. Eisenhower. *Harry*: President Harry S. Truman.

58. "Strike Blues" by John Lee Hooker. Detroit, 1950, Unissued, Specialty 2127, *Goin' Down Highway 51.* © 1970 Venice Music and LaCienga Music Co., c/o ATV Music Corp., BMI; used by permission; all rights reserved.

V I've Been Mistreated

59. "Half a Stranger" by John Lee Hooker. Detroit, 1954, Modern 948, Crown 295, *Folk Blues. Mmmm, etc*: Hooker hums the melody.

60. "Lonesome Home" by "Lightnin' " (Sam) Hopkins. Houston,

1947, Gold Star 624, Kent 523, *Original Folk Blues*. *Raisin' sand*: fussing and fighting.

61. "That Ain't Right" by John Brim. Chicago, 1955, Chess 1588. © 1965 Arc Music, BMI; used by permission. *Loaded*: drunk.

62. "Short Haired Woman" by "Lightnin'" (Sam) Hopkins. Houston, 1947, Unissued take (alternate take issued on Gold Star 313), Verve 8453, *Fast Life Woman*. The alternate take omits verse 3. *Rats*: hairpieces.

63. "Pepper Head Woman" by Square Walton. New York, 1953, Victor 20-5493, Highway 51 104, *I'm Your Country Man*. *I got to beat it out, etc.*: I'm going to play an instrumental break.

64. "Give Me Back That Wig" by "Lightning'" (Sam) Hopkins. Houston, ca. 1951, Crown (LP) 5224, Kent 523, *Original Folk Blues*.

65. "Money Taking Woman" by Johnny Young. Chicago, 1947, Ora-Nelle 712, Blues Classics 8, *Chicago Blues*. *Raise some sand*: fuss and fight.

66. "Big Town Playboy" by Little Johnny Jones. Chicago, 1950, Aristocrat 405. *Lay me some racket* (cue to his accompanists): make some good music now. *Go sharp*: be stylish.

67. "Chicago Blues" by Little Johnny Jones. Chicago, 1953, Unissued, Atlantic 7227, *Blues Piano*.

68. "Black Man Blues," by John Lee Hooker. Detroit, 1948, King 4283, Red Lightnin' 003, *No Friend Around*.

69. "When the Sun is Shining" by L. C. Green. Detroit, 1952, Dot 1103, pwb 5, *Detroit*.

70. "Playing the Races" by John Lee Hooker. Detroit, 1950, Modern 20–730, Kent 9006, *Detroit Blues*. © 1971 Modern Music Publ. Co., BMI; used by permission. *Dreamed a number*: dream objects or events keyed to standard number combinations by various "dream books"; the resulting numbers may be bet on horses or in a numbers lottery using such uncontrollable digits as total sales volume on a stock exchange. In the 1970s, many states instituted legal lotteries.

71. "Long Distance Call" by "Muddy Waters" (McKinley Morganfield). Chicago, 1951, Chess 1452, Chess 1427, *The Best of Muddy Waters*. © 1959 Arc Music Corp., BMI; used by permission. *Another mule kickin' in your stall*: someone else is sleeping with your lover.

72. "Bad Woman Blues" by Eddie Burns. Detroit, 1948, Holiday 202, Blues Classics 23, *Juke Joint Blues*. *Jive*: fool, deceive. *Puttin' down*: giving.

73. Don't Start Me To Talking'" by "Sonny Boy Williamson" (Rice Miller). Chicago, 1955, Checker 824, Argo 4026, *The Blues*. © 1955 Arc Music Corp., BMI; used by permission. *Signifyin'*: tricking; lying. *Get my hair a sock*: hair-straightening treatment.

74. "You Can't Make the Grade" by James "Beale Street" Clark. Chicago, 1946, Columbia 37391, Testament 2207, *Chicago Blues, the Early Years*.

75. "In My Younger Days" by "Sonny Boy Williamson" (Rice Miller). Chicago, 1963, Checker 1080, Chess 1509, *More Real Folk Blues*.

76. "Hoodoo, Hoodoo" by "Sonny Boy" (John Lee) Williamson. Chicago, 1946, Victor 20–2184, Blues Classics 20, *Sonny Boy Williamson, Vol. 2. Knowling*: Ransom Knowling, accompanist on bass. *Mojo hand*: hoodoo love charm. *John*: Blind John Davis, accompanist on piano. *Lacey*: Willie Lacey, accompanist on guitar.

77. "Five Long Years" by Eddie Boyd. Chicago, 1952, J.O.B. 1007, Blues Classics 8, *Chicago Blues*.

78. "Mama's Baby Child" by "Lightnin' " (Sam) Hopkins. Houston, 1948, Imperial 12211, *Lightnin' Hopkins and the Blues*.

79. "What Wrong Have I Done" by "Country Slim" (Ernest Lewis). Los Angeles, 1953, Hollywood 1005, Muskadine 103, *Alla Blues*.

80. "Bad Lover Blues" by "Baby Boy" (Robert) Warren. Detroit, 1954, Sampson 633, Nighthawk 104, *Detroit Ghetto Blues*.

81. "Don't Laugh At Me" by "Howlin' Wolf" (Chester Burnett). Chicago, 1966, Chess 1945, Chess 418, *Change My Way*.

82. "Street Loafin' Woman" by Jimmy McCracklin. Los Angeles, ca. 1946, Globe 109, Muskadine 104, *Unfinished Boogie. Jay*: J. D. Nicholson, accompanist on piano. *Beat out some blues now*: play the piano well. *Pallet*: bed.

83. "Gypsy Woman" by "Muddy Waters" (McKinley Morganfield). Chicago, 1947, Aristocrat 1302, Genesis 6641 047, *The Beginnings of Rock*.

84. "Peace Breaking People" by "Lil' Son" (Melvin) Jackson. Los Angeles, 1950, Imperial 5113. *Peace breaking people*: gossips.

85. "Nervy Woman Blues" by "Baby Boy" (Robert) Warren. Detroit, 1949, Staff 706, Kingfish 1001, *Detroit Blues*.

VI I'm Gonna Have to Let Her Go

86. "Fattening Frogs For Snakes" by "Sonny Boy Williamson" (Rice Miller). Chicago, 1957, Checker 864. © 1964 Arc Music Corp., BMI; used by permission.

87. "Smoke Stack Lightning" by "Howlin' Wolf" (Chester Burnett). Chicago, 1956, Chess 1618, Chess 1434, *Moanin' in the Moonlight*. © 1956 Arc Music Corp., BMI; used by permission. The title is probably a corruption of the traditional line, "Well the smokestack is black and the bell it shine like gold," describing a railroad steam-engine. Charley Patton,

from whom Wolf learned several lyrics, sang that line in his 1930 recording of "Moon Going Down"; undoubtedly, Wolf heard him sing it in many different songs.

88. "Locked Out Boogie" by Leroy Foster. Chicago, 1949, Aristocrat 1234. © 1972 Arc Music Corp., BMI; used by permission. *Dozens*: verbal game of wits in which players take turns ridiculing each others' ancestry by insulting relatives.

89. "Mistreated Blues" by Buddy Chiles. Houston, 1949, Gold Star 660, pwb 4, *Texas*. *Dog me*: treat like a dog or other dumb animal.

90. "Moonshine Blues" by "Little Walter" (Walter Jacobs). Chicago, 1950, Parkway 502. *Whiskey-headed*: alcoholic. *High brownskin*: woman of light brown complexion.

91. "Dog Me Around" by "Howlin' Wolf" (Chester Burnett). Memphis, ca. 1948, Kent 526, *Original Folk Blues*. © 1974 Modern Music Publ. Co., BMI; used by permission. Wolf remade this song in 1951 as "How Many More Years" (Chess 1479) but the earlier version is superior.

92. "Ludella" by "Jimmy Rogers" (James A. Lane). Chicago, 1949, Unissued, Biograph 12035, *Love Changin' Blues*. Rogers remade this song in 1950 under the same title (Chess 1435) but the earlier version is superior.

93. "Best Days" by "Baby Face" Turner. N. Little Rock, 1952(?) Unissued, Kent 9007, *Arkansas Blues*. © 1971 Modern Music Publ. Co., BMI; used by permission.

94. "Hole in the Wall" by L. C. Williams. Houston, 1948, Gold Star 623, Blues Classics 16, *Texas Blues*. *Raisin' sand*: fussing and fighting.

95. "Bad Life Blues" by "Smokey" (Andrew) Hogg. Los Angeles, 1948, Unissued, Kent 9005, *Texas Blues*.

96. "I'm Leavin' You Baby" by "Lightnin' Slim" (Otis Hicks). Crowley, Louisiana, 1959, Excello 2150, Excello 8000, *Rooster Blues*. © 1959 Excellorec Music Co., BMI; used by permission.

97. "Just Can't Stay" by Willie Nix. Chicago, 1953, Sabre 104, Boogie Disease 101–102, *Take a Little Walk with Me*. *Trash*: flattery.

98. "I'm Gonna Quit You, Baby" by Silas Hogan. Crowley, Louisiana, ca. 1962, Excello 2231, Blue Horizon 2431 008, *Trouble at Home*. *Raisin' sand*: fussing and fighting.

99. "So Long Blues" by Silas Hogan. Crowley, Louisiana, ca. 1965, Excello 2270, Blue Horizon 2431 008, *Trouble at Home*. © 1965 Excellorec Music, BMI; used by permission.

100. "One Of These Days" by "Big Boy" (Arthur) Spires. Chicago, 1952, Checker 752, Chess 411, *Drop Down Mama*. © 1970 Arc Music Corp., BMI; used by permission.

101. "Wednesday Evenin' Blues" by John Lee Hooker. Chicago, 1961, Vee Jay (LP) 1003, Archive of Folk and Jazz 222, *John Lee Hooker*. Hooker

first recorded this title for Modern in 1948 but it was unissued. He recorded it once again in 1960 for Riverside and its folk-revival andience, but that version is inferior to the one transcribed here.

102. "No Nights By Myself" by "Sonny Boy Williamson" (Rice Miller). Jackson, Mississippi, 1954, Ace 511.

103. "You Can't Tell Them Where I'm Going" by "Smokey" (Andrew) Hogg. Los Angeles, ca 1950, Kent 5024, *Original Folk Blues*.

104. "I Tried" by Sylvester Cotton. Detroit, 1949, Modern 893 (issued as by John Lee Hooker), Kent 9006, *Detroit Blues*.© 1971 Modern Music Publ. Co., BMI; used by permission. *Brunie Besman*: Bernie Besman, record producer.

105. "Got To Let You Go" by Joe Hill Louis. Memphis, 1950, Phillips 9001, Nighthawk 103, *Low Down Memphis Harmonica Jam*. *Caldonia*: stock character in black American humor, a very slow-witted woman. *The be-bop boy*: this singer's nickname.

106. "I Better Go Now" "Howlin' Wolf" (Chester Burnett). Chicago, 1958, Chess 1726, Chess 418, *Change My Way*.

107. "Crying Won't Help You" "Tampa Red" (Hudson Whittaker). Chicago, 1946, Victor 20–1988, Blues Classics 25, *The Guitar Wizard*. *Dig these jives, etc.*: Listen to this fine instrumental break.

108. "Early Morning" by Floyd Jones. Chicago, 1952, Chess 1527, Nighthawk 102, *Chicago Slickers*.

109. "Train Time" by "Sunnyland Slim" (Albert Luandrew). Chicago, 1953, Opera 5, Nighthawk 102, *Chicago Slickers*.

110. "Take It Easy Baby" by "Robert Nighthawk" (Robert McCullum). Chicago, 1951, Unissued, Pearl 11, *Bricks in My Pillow*. *Cold in hand*: broke, penniless.

111. "Goin' Down Highway 51" by John Lee Hooker. Detroit, ca. 1949, Unissued, Specialty 2127, *Goin' Down Highway 51*.© 1970 Venice Music and LaCienega Music Co., c/o ATV Music Corp., BMI, used by permission; all rights reserved. *B. & O.* Baltimore and Ohio Railroad.

112. "Bye Bye Bird" by "Sonny Boy Williamson" (Rice Miller). Chicago. 1962, Unissued, Rarity 1, *Last Session*.

VII Sometime I Was Goin' So Fast That I Just Couldn't See The Road

113. "Hard Times" by Johnny Fuller. Oakland, California, 1954, Flair 1054, Kent 9003, *California Blues*.© 1970 Modern Music Publ. Co., BMI; used by permission.

114. "I Can't Be Satisfied" by "Muddy Waters" (McKinley Morgan-

field). Chicago, 1948, Aristocrat 1305, Chess 1427, *The Best of Muddy Waters*. © 1959 Arc Music Corp., BMI; used by permission.

115. "Down Home Girl" by "Memphis Minnie" (Minnie McCoy Lawlar). Chicago, 1949, Unissued, Biograph 12035, *Love Changin' Blues*.

116. "The End" by James Reed. Oakland, California, 1954, Flair 1034, Kent 9003, *California Blues*. © 1970 Modern Music Publ. Co., BMI; used by permission.

117. "On The Road Again" by Floyd Jones. Chicago, 1953, J.O.B. 1013, Muskadine 1, *On the Road Again*. *Sunnyland*: Sunnyland Slim (Albert Luandrew), piano accompanist.

118. "Grievance Blues" by "Lightnin' " (Sam) Hopkins. Houston, 1949, Gold Star 673, Arhoolie 2006, *Texas Blues*.

119. "Falling Rain Blues" by Little Willie Foster. Chicago, 1953, Blue Lake 113, Blues Classics 8, *Chicago Blues*. *Floyd*: Floyd Jones, accompanist on guitar. *Dynaflow*: Buick automobile.

120. "Goin' Back and Talk to Mama" by "Lightnin' " (Sam) Hopkins. Houston, ca. 1947, Unissued, Arhoolie 2007, *Original Recordings, Vol. 1*.

121. "Shelby County Blues" by Little Johnny Jones. Chicago, 1950, Aristocrat 405. *Shelby County*: Memphis Tenn. *Kid*: young lover. *Boogie-assed*: eager for sex.

122. "Seventy-Four Blues" by Willie Love. Jackson, Mississippi, 1951, Trumpet 173, Blues Classics 15, *Memphis and the Delta*. *Cold in hand*: empty-handed; broke, penniless.

123. "The Goat" by "Sonny Boy Williamson" (Rice Miller). Chicago, 1959, Checker 943, Chess 1509, *More Real Folk Blues*. © 1960 Arc Music Corp., BMI; used by permission.

124. "Louisiana Blues" by "Muddy Waters" (McKinley Morganfield). Chicago, 1950, Chess 1441, Chess 1427, *The Best of Muddy Waters*. © 1959 Arc Music Corp., BMI; used by permission. *Mojo hand*: love charm.

125. "Good Evening Everybody" by "Sonny Boy Williamson" (Rice Miller). Chicago, 1955, Unissued, Chess 417, *One Way Out*. © 1976 Arc Music Corp., BMI; used by permission.

Notes and References

Preface

1. Harry Oster. *Living Country Blues* (Hatboro, Pa.: Folklore Associates, 1969). The lyrics sung by Robert Pete Williams and collected by Oster are eccentric in the blues tradition but from a literary viewpoint rank with the outstanding lyrics in the present anthology.

2. Eric Sackheim and Jonathan Shahn, *The Blues Line* (1969; rpt., New York: Schirmer Books, 1975).

Introduction

1. "The most expressive music of any given period will be an exact reflection of what the Negro himself is." LeRoi Jones, *Blues People* (New York: William Morrow, 1963), p. 137.

2. Stephen Henderson, *Understanding the New Black Poetry* (New York: William Morrow, 1973).

3. Eileen Southern, *The Music of Black Americans* (New York: Norton, 1971) is standard. Gilbert Chase, *America's Music* (Rev. 2nd ed., New York: McGraw-Hill, 1966) is the outstanding one-volume history of American music. A third edition is in preparation and will be published shortly by the University of Illinois Press.

4. Cleanth Brooks, R. W. B. Lewis, and Robert Penn Warren, eds., *American Literature: The Makers and the Making* (New York: St. Martin's, 1973).

5. An excellent summary of modern folklore theory and its application to folksong, oral literature, and material culture may be found in Barre Toelken's ground-breaking textbook, *The Dynamics of Folklore* (Boston: Houghton-Mifflin, 1979).

6. See Jeff Titon, *Early Downhome Blues* (Urbana: University of Illinois Press, 1977), pp. xv, 57–59.

7. Lightnin' (Sam) Hopkins, "Candy Kitchen." Musical transcription by author.

8. Jimmy Rogers, "Money, Marbles and Chalk." Musical transcription by author.

9. See *Early Downhome Blues*, pp. 155–161, for a discussion of the *blue note*.

10. Ibid., chapter 4.

11. Ibid., chapter 1, pp. 24–30.

12. See, for example, Howard Odum, "Folk-Song and Folk-Poetry as Found in the Secular Songs of the Southern Negroes," *Journal of American Folklore* 24 (July-Sept. 1911), pp. 255–294; 25 (Oct.-Dec. 1911) pp. 351–396. Odum collected these songs between 1905 and 1908.

13. See *Early Downhome Blues*, chapter 6, for a discussion of blues recording in the 1920s.

14. Paul Oliver, *The Story of the Blues* (New York: Chilton Book Co., 1974).

15. Mike Rowe, *Chicago Breakdown* (London: Eddison Press, 1973), p. 65.

16. James Rooney, *Bossmen: Bill Monroe and Muddy Waters* (New York: Hayden Book Co., 1971), p. 107.

17. Rooney, *Bossmen*, pp. 105–107.

18. These recordings made for the Library of Congress have been issued on *Muddy Waters: Down on Stovall's Plantation* (Testament T 2210).

19. Peter Guralnick, *Feel Like Going Home* (New York: Outerbridge and Dienstfrey, 1971), p. 47.

20. Rooney, *Bossmen* p. 110.

21. Jeff Titon, "Calling All Cows: Lazy Bill Lucas, part 2," *Blues Unlimited*, No. 61 (April 1969), p. 10.

22. Rowe, *Chicago*, p. 71.

23. Jeff Titon, *From Blues to Pop: The Autobiography of Leonard "Baby Doo" Caston* (Los Angeles: John Edwards Memorial Foundation, Special Series, No. 4, 1974), p. 27.

24. Lightnin' Hopkins, " Tim Moore's Farm" (transcription 5). In the interests of economy I quote only those lines necessary for illustration.

25. J. B. Hutto, "Things Are So Slow" (transcription 52).

26. Johnny Young, "Money Taking Woman" (transcription 65).

27. L. C. Williams, "Hole in the Wall" (transcription 94).

28. Eddie Burns, "Bad Woman Blues" (transcription 72).

29. John Lee Hooker, "Black Man Blues" (transcription 68).

30. Nat Terry, "Take It Easy Baby" (transcription 39).

31. Sonny Boy Williamson, "Your Funeral and My Trial" (transcription 42).

32. Sonny Boy Williamson, "This Old Life" (transcription 41).

33. Floyd Jones, "Stockyard Blues" (transcription 51).

34. John Brim, "Tough Times" (transcription 53).

35. Lightnin' Hopkins, "Lonesome Home" (transcription 60).

36. John Lee Hooker, "Black Man Blues" (transcription 68).

37. Buddy Chiles, "Mistreated Blues" (transcription 89), complete text.

38. Baby Face Turner, "Best Days" (transcription 93).

39. Howlin' Wolf, "Dog Me Around" (transcription 91).

40. Sonny Boy Williamson, "Fattening Frogs for Snakes" (transcription 86).

41. L. C. Williams, "Hole in the Wall" (transcription 94).

42. Eddie Boyd, "Five Long Years" (transcription 77), complete text. The first verse takes the three-line form; the second, third, and fourth verses take the quatrain-refrain form.

43. Lightnin' Hopkins, "Tim Moore's Farm" (transcription 5).

44. Lightnin' Hopkins, "Candy Kitchen" (transcription 56), complete text.

A Basic Record Library of Postwar Downhome Blues

It is not as difficult now as it was fifteen years ago to build a library of postwar downhome blues recordings because most of the outstanding performances have been reissued from their original 78 or 45 rpm singles and gathered on LP albums. Some of these reissue albums have gone out of print only to reappear a few years later under new titles and different release numbers, while others have remained out of print. Performances on several of the reissue albums are often duplicated on others. Nonetheless, many excellent albums are available; others, particularly those currently out of print on the Chess label will probably reappear once more in the near future.

The best way to build a collection is to concentrate on two types of reissue albums: anthologies and albums wholly given over to outstanding single artists. The anthologies usually focus on a geographical region or city that was a center for postwar downhome blues. Albums devoted to single artists can suffer from a sameness of musical accompaniment but they offer an in-depth portrait of the artist.

This list of recommended albums includes only those which feature downhome blues songs originally made on commercial 78s and 45s and marketed primarily in the black communities. This reflects the limits I imposed upon myself in selecting the lyrics for this book. The listing omits other types of postwar blues albums, many of them excellent: (1) on-location field recordings made for the Library of Congress and other folk music archives; (2) studio-made albums (not reissues from singles) presenting the blues artists as folk singers for white, middle-class audiences; (3) albums featuring white singers and bands; and (4) reissues of urban blues 78s and 45s by such artists as Wynonie Harris, T-Bone Walker, B. B. King, and Charles Brown.

Most of the albums listed are (or were) issued by American record companies. Those marked with an asterisk (*) were out of print at publication of this book but they can often be found in used record stores and "cut-out" bins.

Anthologies

Chicago

Blues Is Killing Me. Juke Joint 1501. Jones, Foster, Lenoir, Brim, etc.
Chicago Blues. Blues Classics 8. Foster, Hutto, Boyd, Jones, and Young.
Chicago Blues: The Beginning. Testament 2207. Waters, Shines—1940s.
Chicago Slickers. Nighthawk 102. Jones, Brim, Shines, Nighthawk, etc.
*Drop Down Mama. Chess 411. Jones, Shines, Nighthawk, Spires, etc.
On the Road Again. Muskadine 100. Jones, Shines, etc.
*Take a Little Walk with Me. Boogie Disease 101/102. Nix, Jones, Brim, Foster, Young, and Shines.

     See also under *Single Artists*: Crudup, Howlin' Wolf, Memphis Minnie, James, Nighthawk, Reed, Rogers, Tampa Red, Little Walter, Muddy Waters, and Sonny Boy Williamson.

West Coast

Alla Blues. Muskadine 103. Lewis, Johnson, etc.
California Blues. United 7780. Reed, Fuller, Watson, etc.; formerly packaged under same title, as *Kent 9003.
Oakland Blues. Arhoolie 2008. Dee, Fuller, etc.
West Coast Blues. United 7789. Dee, Reed, etc.; formerly packaged under same title, as *Kent 9012.

See also under *Single Artists*: Fulson, Hogg, and Sims.

Texas

Texas Blues. Arhoolie 2006. Jackson and Hopkins.
Texas Blues. Blues Classics 16. Dee, Sims, Hopkins, Hogg, and Williams.

See also under *Single Artists*: Fulson, Hogg, and Hopkins.

Memphis and the Mississippi Delta.

*Arkansas Blues. Kent 9007. Turner, Blair, and Brooks.
The Blues Came Down from Memphis. Charly 30125. Ross, Cotton, Nix, etc.; British LP, formerly packaged under same title, as *London HAS 8265.

Memphis and the Delta. Blues Classics 15. Love, Turner, Gilmore, and
  Louis.
Mississippi Blues. United 7786. Gilmore, Boines, Booker, etc.; formerly
  packaged under same title, as *Kent 9009.

See also under *Single Artists*: Hogan, Hooker, Howlin' Wolf, Lightnin'
Slim, Lonesome Sundown, Doctor Ross, and Sonny Boy Williamson.

Detroit

Blues Guitar Killers. Barrelhouse 012. Green.
Detroit Blues. Blues Classics 12. Warren, Ross, Hooker, and Green.
Detroit Blues. United 7783. Hooker, S. Cotton, etc.; formerly packaged
  under same title, as *Kent 9006.
Detroit Ghetto Blues.Nighthawk 104. Green, Warren, etc.

See also under *Single Artists*: Hooker and Warren.

East Coast

Play My Jukebox. Flyright 4711. Pickett, Weaver, etc.; British LP.

See also under *Single Artists*: Howard and Seward.

Single Artists

Crudup, Arthur. *Father of Rock and Roll.* RCA LPV 573.
Fulson, Lowell. *Hung Down Head.* Chess 408.
Hogan, Silas. *Trouble at Home.* Excello 8019.
Hogg, Smokey. *Original Folk Blues.* United 7745.
Hooker, John Lee. *Moanin' and Stompin' the Blues.* King 1085.
_____. *Going Down Highway 51.* Specialty 2127.
_____. *The Blues.* United 7725.
Hopkins, Sam "Lightnin'." *Early Recordings*, Vols. 1 and 2. Arhoolie 2007,
  2010.
_____. *The Blues.* Mainstream 311.
_____. *Original Folk Blues.* United 7744. Formerly packaged under same
  title, as *Kent 523.

————. *A Legend in His Own Time.* United 7785. Formerly packaged under same title, as *Kent 9008.

Howard, Paul. *Faded Picture Blues.* King 1098.

Howlin' Wolf (Chester Burnett). *Big City Blues.* United 7177. Formerly packaged under same title, as *Kent 526.

————. *Change My Way.* Chess 418.

————. *Howlin' Wolf.* Two LPs, much duplication with the following three earlier albums. Chess 2 ACMB 201.

————. *Evil.* Chess 1540. Repackaging of *Moanin' in the Moonlight.* Chess 1434.

————. *Howlin' Wolf.* Chess 1469.

————. *The Real Folk Blues.* Chess 1502.

James, Elmore. *Whose Muddy Shoes. Chess 1537.* Also includes several songs by John Brim.

Lightnin' Slim (Otis Hicks). *Lightnin' Slim's Bell Ringer.* Excello 8004.

Little Walter (Walter Jacobs). *Little Walter.* Chess 2 ACMB 202. Two LPs. Duplication with the following three earlier albums.

————. *Boss Blues Harmonica.* Chess 2 CH 60014. Two LPs, including a repackaging of *The Best of Little Walter.* Checker 3004.

————. *Confessin' the Blues.* Chess 416.

————. *Hate to See You Go.* Chess 1535.

Lonesome Sundown (Cornelius Green). *Lonesome Sundown.* Excello 8012.

Memphis Minnie (Minnie Douglas McCoy Lawlar). *Love Changin' Blues.* Biograph 12035. Her best recordings appeared prior to WWII and are available on *Memphis Minnie,* Vols. 1 and 2. Blues Classics 1 and 13.

Nighthawk, Robert (Robert McCullum). *Bricks in My Pillow.* Pearl 11.

Reed, Jimmy. *The Ultimate Jimmy Reed.* ABC Bluesway 6067.

Rogers, Jimmy. *Jimmy Rogers.* Chess 2 ACMB 207. Two LPs, including a repackaging of *Chicago Bound,* Chess 407.

Ross, Doctor. *Doctor Ross: His Original Recordings.* Arhoolie 1065.

Seward, Alec. *Guitar Slim and Jelly Belly.* Arhoolie 2005.

Sims, Frankie Lee. *Lucy Mae Blues.* Specialty 2124.

Tampa Red (Hudson Whittaker). *The Guitar Wizard.* Blues Classics 25.

Warren, Baby Boy. *Detroit Blues.* Kingfish 1001.

Waters, Muddy (McKinley Morganfield). *Back in the Early Days.* Syndicate Chapter 001/002. British, 2 LPs.

————. *Muddy Waters.* Chess 2 ACMB 203. Two LPs, including a repackaging of *Sail On,* Chess 1539, which was a repackaging of *The Best of Muddy Waters.* Chess 1472. Much duplication with the following album as well.

————. *The Real Folk Blues.* Chess 1501.

_____. *They Call Me Muddy Waters*. Chess 1553.

Williamson, Sonny Boy (Rice Miller, not to be confused with John Lee "Sonny Boy" Wiliamson, who died in 1948). *King Biscuit Time*. Arhoolie 2020. Formerly packaged as *The Original Sonny Boy Williamson*. Blues Classic 9.

_____. *Sonny Boy Williamson*. Chess 2 ACMB 206. Two LPs, much duplication with the following three albums.

_____. *The Real Folk Blues*. Chess 1503.

_____. *More Real Folk Blues*. Chess 1509.

_____. *Bummer Road*. Chess 1536.

_____. *One Way Out*. Chess 417.

Suggestions for Further Reading

Books

Ferris, William. *Blues from the Delta.* Garden City, N.Y.: Doubleday, 1978. 226 p.
An introduction to contemporary folk blues in the Mississippi Delta based on field collecting; contains transcribed excerpts from blues performances at a house party, where the informal atmosphere has an important effect on the songs.
Gilett, Charlie. *The Sound of the City: the Rise of Rock and Roll.* New York: Outerbridge and Dienstfrey, 1970. 178 p.
Chapter 6 contains a useful discussion of postwar urban blues.
Groom, Bob. *The Blues Revival.* London: Studio Vista, 1971. 112 p.
A history of the resurging interest in blues music during the past 25 years and the researchers who were partly responsible for it.
Guralnick, Peter. *Feel Like Going Home: Portraits in Blues & Rock 'n' Roll.* New York: Outerbridge and Dienstfrey, 1971. 224 p.
Sympathetic, knowledgeable, and factually accurate sketches of the personalities and careers of Muddy Waters, Johnny Shines, Robert Pete Williams, Howlin' Wolf, and the Chess Brothers.
Haralambos, Michael. *Right On: From Blues to Soul in Black America.* London: Eddison Press, 1974. 187 p.
Working with LeRoi Jones's thesis (from *Blues People*) that black popular music reflects black social consciousness, Haralambos argues that the blues is accommodative whereas soul music reflects the 1960s shift to social solidarity and protest.
Jones, LeRoi. *Blues People.* New York: William Morrow, 1963. 244p.
Thought-provoking history of black American music with an emphasis on the blues; also contains a perspective which contrasts "people's music" (folk music) with media-manipulated popular music.
Keil, Charles. *Urban Blues.* Chicago: University of Chicago Press, 1966. 231 p.

Energetic, perceptive analysis of the socio-cultural impact of the black popular music industry in the 1960s: singers, disc jockeys, record producers, and audience.

Leadbitter, Mike, ed. *Nothing but the Blues.* London: Hanover Books; New York: Oak Publication, 1971. 278 p.

Contains much biographical information about downhome blues singers, many from the postwar era, culled from articles in *Blues Unlimited,* 1963–1969. The American edition provides a useful index.

Leadbitter, Mike, and **Slaven, Neal** eds. *Blues Records, 1943–1966.* London: Hanover Books, 1968; New York: Oak Publications, 1970. 381 p.

The only postwar blues discography. Contains the following information on more than ten thousand recordings: singer, title, accompanists, record company, recording date, matrix number, and release number. A revised edition is underway.

Oakley, Giles. *The Devil's Music: a History of the Blues.* New York: Harcourt, Brace, Jovanovich, 1976. 287 p.

Written to accompany a British Broadcasting Company (BBC) television series on the blues; a sound introduction to the historical development of downhome blues.

Oliver, Paul. *Conversation with the Blues.* London: Cassell & Co., 1965. 217 p.

Brief interviews with several blues singers that Oliver met on a field trip in 1960.

——————. *The Story of the Blues.* London: Barrie & Rockliffe, 1969; New York: Chilton Book Co., 1974. 177 p.

Good survey of downhome blues, with emphasis on the prewar era. Includes much thoroughly-researched biographical information, perceptive analysis, and intriguing photos.

Oster, Harry. *Living Country Blues.* Detroit: Folklore Associates, 1969. 430 p.

Analysis and texts of more than 200 folk blues songs collected by folklorist Oster in Louisiana in the mid- to late-1950s. Contains several memorable lyrics, especially by Robert Pete Williams. Highly recommended.

Rooney, James. *Bossmen: Bill Monroe and Muddy Waters.* New York: Hayden Book Co., 1971. 159 p.

Lengthy interview with Waters punctuated by Rooney's interpretive comments. (Monroe is the "father" of bluegrass music.)

Rowe, Mike. *Chicago Breakdown.* London: Eddison Press, 1973. 226 p.

This history of blues in Chicago concentrates on the post-war era and is a useful compendium of information about many of the singers whose lyrics appear in this collection.

Sackheim, Eric, and Shahn, Jonathan. *The Blues Line: A Collection of Blues Lyrics*. New York: Grossman Publishers, 1969; reprinted, New York: Schirmer Books, 1975. 499 p.

Transcriptions of nearly 300 downhome blues lyrics, all but a dozen or so from the prewar era. A reliable companion to this anthology.

Titon, Jeff Todd. *Early Downhome Blues: A Musical and Cultural Analysis*. Urbana: University of Illinois Press, 1977; Illini paperback, 1979. 296 p.

Ethnomusicological treatment of downhome blues in the prewar era; contains some technical musical analysis.

Periodicals

Much of the information published in these two research journals has become outdated and the writing is often more appropriate for fan magazines. However, the periodicals remain useful for biographical information and record reviews.

Blues Unlimited, 8 Brandram Way, Lewisham, London, England. Approximately bi-monthly since 1963.

Living Blues, 2615 N. Wilton Ave., Chicago, Illinois, 60614. Quarterly from 1970–1974; bi-monthly since 1975. Many lengthy, valuable interviews with singers.

See also:

Southern Folklore Quarterly, 42, no. 1 (1978). Special blues issue, with analytical articles contributed by folklorists and ethnomusicologists.

Index of Singers' Names

Index of Song Titles